Transitional Justice

D0863004

Transitional Justice

Contending with the Past

Michael Newman

polity

First published in 2019 by Polity Press

Polity Press
65 Bridge Street
Cambridge CB2 1UR, UK

Polity Press
101 Station Landing
Suite 300
Medford, MA 02155, USA

ISBN-13: 978-1-5095-2115-9
ISBN-13: 978-1-5095-2116-6 (pb)

A catalogue record for this book is available from the British Library.

Library of Congress Cataloging-in-Publication Data

Names: Newman, Michael, 1946- author.
Title: Transitional justice : contending with the past / Michael Newman.
Description: Cambridge, UK ; Medford, MA, USA : Polity Press, [2019] |
    Includes bibliographical references and index.
Identifiers: LCCN 2018048567 (print) | LCCN 2018061767 (ebook) | ISBN
    9781509521197 (Epub) | ISBN 9781509521159 | ISBN 9781509521166 (pb)
Subjects: LCSH: Transitional justice.
Classification: LCC K5250 (ebook) | LCC K5250 .N49 2019 (print) | DDC
    340/.115--dc23
LC record available at https://lccn.loc.gov/2018048567

Typeset in 11 on 13 pt Sabon by Fakenham Prepress Solutions, Fakenham, Norfolk NR21 8NL
Printed and bound in the UK by CPI Group (UK) Ltd, Croydon

For further information on Polity, visit our website: politybooks.com

Contents

Preface

What does a new regime do in the aftermath of mass atrocities committed by a brutal dictatorship? How can a society overcome the traumatic past of a violent civil war and move forward to a peaceful future? Is it possible to establish a just settlement in which past wrongs are acknowledged and addressed? These are central questions in what is now known as 'transitional justice' (TJ), but this field is highly contested.

TJ is most frequently viewed as a set of mechanisms or tools, which typically include criminal prosecutions of perpetrators of mass human rights abuses; truth commissions to investigate exactly what happened; reparation programmes for victims and survivors; and memorials and education. When implemented singly or in combination, these often capture the attention of people who may not be familiar with the term. For example, long after its completion in 1998, the South African Truth and Reconciliation Commission remains widely familiar, and, by discussing it, those outside the TJ community quickly become engaged in debates as to whether truth commissions, trials, amnesties or other mechanisms are the most appropriate way to deal with mass abuses and violations associated with former regimes or civil wars. Such issues will be considered throughout the book, but its subtitle, 'Contending with the Past', in my view, highlights an element that is still more fundamental to TJ than any set of mechanisms.

'Contending' in this context suggests the idea of struggling to surmount something that is inherently difficult, and TJ necessarily occurs in such circumstances. After mass abuses, atrocities or other forms of injustice, it is inevitable that a transition will be problematic, for the legacy of such violations will continue far beyond the establishment of a new regime or government. Contending with the past implies a genuine struggle to overcome this legacy, and this is not at all common. Historically, many transitional regimes have remained silent about the past, and Spain is often cited as a comparatively recent example of this. In 1939 General Franco defeated republican and left-wing forces after a brutal civil war and then ruled in a dictatorship until his death in late 1975. But the new regime decided to draw a veil over the long period of violence and repression. This followed from a belief that instituting measures to bring about accountability, or even serious discussions of recent history, would make it impossible to create a stable society.

Subsequently the international climate changed, and since the 1990s there has been an increasing expectation and demand that, in the aftermath of mass abuses, new regimes or governments will introduce some of the measures associated with TJ. But contending with the past is certainly not guaranteed by the implementation of a set of mechanisms, which may be promulgated superficially or at the behest of external forces, or even cynically to divert attention from continuing injustices. Furthermore, it is quite typical for both new and existing regimes to create myths about the past as a means of legitimating a current status quo and set of prevailing attitudes. Thus, in the UK, and particularly England, history has often been used selectively and in a celebratory way, constantly harking back to the Second World War, rather than also confronting the reality of an imperial past built on violence, racism and economic pillage. Suggesting that TJ means genuinely contending with the past is therefore to set it high goals which may rarely be achieved in practice. But I take it that this objective must be an integral part of its aspirations if it is to mean more than implementing a set of tools. What, then, is the nature of this book?

One reflection of the exponential growth in the field has been the extent of academic and practitioner publications devoted to TJ. In the early years, it tended to be regarded as a branch of law, but subsequently it has been taken up by a whole range of other disciplines and subject areas – most obviously, politics and international relations, but also peace and conflict studies, philosophy, sociology, anthropology and others, including history, cultural studies and education. This concise work seeks to encapsulate many of the key issues and debates in TJ, drawing on a variety of cases. It also raises fundamental questions about the nature and assumptions of conventional TJ and discusses critical approaches to the concept and practice. It is necessarily highly selective, but it seeks to provide an illustrative overview which will simultaneously open up the subject and a sense of its importance to those coming to it for the first time, while offering new insights and food for thought to those already familiar with it.

Acknowledgements

I am grateful to the staff at Polity Press, and particularly to George Owers, for so readily accepting my proposal and for his editorial suggestions throughout the process. The comments of four anonymous reviewers were very helpful, and I am pleased to acknowledge their work. I also want to thank Christine Bell for devising the phrase 'contending with the past' as the most appropriate description of transitional justice and for supporting my use of it as the subtitle in this book. My thanks also go to Par Engstrom, Rachel Kerr, Iavor Rangelov and the late Chandra Lekha Sriram for the stimulating seminars through the London Transitional Justice Network, and to the staff at New York University in London for providing a friendly and helpful environment for teaching and research. Once again I really appreciate my brother Jeff's general interest in the book as well as his careful reading of the text. Above all, as always, I cannot thank Ines enough for her constant encouragement and support and for being such a brilliant constructive critic.

1

Introducing
Transitional Justice

Transitional justice (TJ) appeared as a term and arguably also as a concept only very recently, but its pace of development has been remarkable. In academic terms, this has been demonstrated by the proliferation of research institutes and university courses devoted to the topic, with a sample of 150 academic institutions in 2015 (half in the US and half across the world) revealing that almost 50 per cent taught a TJ-related course (Reiter and Surian 2015). However, it is obviously not solely an academic field, and there has been an equally rapid growth in TJ as a set of practices. As a reflection of both academic and practitioner involvement, in 2007 a new specialist journal, the *International Journal for Transitional Justice*, was launched, followed five years later by a second, *Transitional Justice Review*. Yet there are many debates and disputes about the ways in which TJ should be defined, theorised and practised.

This chapter begins by examining the emergence and development of TJ and then considers questions of definition and conceptualisation. It highlights differing strands of opinion within the field and raises many questions and points of contention that will be discussed more fully in later parts of the book. The second chapter turns to a consideration of some of the principal mechanisms through which TJ has been put into practice.

Origins and Development

The term itself may be extremely recent, but this does not tell us whether it is also a new concept or whether it can be traced back historically. Some scholars have argued that ancient Athens might provide an early example (Elster 2004; Lanni 2014). Following the defeat of Athens in the Peloponnesian War in 404 BCE, a pro-Spartan regime, known as the rule of the Thirty Tyrants, maintained power for eight months and instituted highly repressive measures, including mass executions, murder and forced exile. The subsequent restoration of Athenian democracy meant that the new government needed to decide how to deal with the tyrants, and it is certainly possible to argue that the mixture of retribution, forgiveness and reconciliation that they instituted foreshadowed late twentieth-century practices. Yet it seems anachronistic to suggest that TJ existed in the distant past, when it emerged as a self-conscious idea and set of values and goals so recently.

A more influential notion has been to argue that the first generation of TJ, or Phase I (Teitel 2003), was established in the aftermath of the Second World War, most notably in the Nuremberg and Tokyo trials. These international trials incorporated the notion of responsibility by German and Japanese individuals for the mass abuses and atrocities, retrospectively deeming them to be war crimes, crimes against humanity and genocide. Such principles would reappear in the canon of TJ at the end of the century, implying continuity with Nuremberg and Tokyo. This was reinforced with the establishment of the International Criminal Tribunal for the former Yugoslavia and that for Rwanda following the mass violations perpetrated in these countries in the 1990s and, still further, with the establishment of the International Criminal Court (ICC) in 2002, with its mandate to prosecute cases of war crimes, crimes against humanity and genocide.

Yet there are also good reasons for questioning the strength of the links between Phase I and a second generation, or Phase II, associated with the 1980s and 1990s. Firstly, despite the importance of the principles set out at Nuremberg, the *primary* rationale of these trials was for the victors to prosecute the vanquished, while most proponents of TJ have sought to justify it through a more elevated set of principles. Secondly, the claim is rather dubious in historical terms, as there were also many discontinuities in the intervening period, with highly repressive regimes often overthrown or falling without any kind of accountability for the abuses that they had perpetrated. Thirdly, the emphasis on continuity through international criminal law serves to uphold a particular interpretation of TJ in which legal institutions and the notion of individual responsibility are accorded particular significance. However, there is considerable agreement about the timing and initial location of 'second-generation' TJ: Latin America in the 1980s and early 1990s, followed quickly by internationalisation, with South Africa playing a pivotal role in this process. But this does not mean that there was any consensus in identifying the most important elements within TJ. This may be illustrated with particular reference to Argentina, which was significant in the origins of this second phase.

Between March 1976 and December 1983, successive military dictators in Argentina sought to eliminate the left through a so-called Dirty War against the social base of two revolutionary guerrilla groups – the Montoneros, an urban group, and the Revolutionary People's Army, which operated mainly in the countryside. In April 1977, a group of fourteen mothers (subsequently known as the Madres de Plaza de Mayo), who had met in police stations while trying to find out what had happened to their children, organised the first of a continuing series of weekly demonstrations in this plaza in Buenos Aires, demanding to know the fate of the victims. This was courageous, and some of the members of the movement, including its first president, themselves 'disappeared'. In spite of this, their numbers grew to several thousands by 1982–3, with a national network, including human rights activists and lawyers, and they also secured international support through such organisations as Amnesty International and the UN Human Rights Commission. One important strand of opinion suggests that this kind of grassroots movement, calling for action against impunity, constitutes the core of TJ (Nesiah 2016). But by 1983 the activists and campaigners were also demanding legal action, and following the fall of the Junta they participated actively in the electoral campaigns of various candidates and parties, staging large demonstrations to repudiate the military's proposal for an amnesty law. In December 1983, the new president, Raúl Alfonsín, signed a decree initiating legal proceedings against nine military officers. A second strand of opinion, which would soon become dominant, has viewed trials and prosecutions as the key element in TJ (Sikkink 2011).

Simultaneously, though, Argentina contributed to the emergence of the truth commission (TC) as a further major component within TJ, because Alfonsín also established a Commission on the Disappeared (*Comisión Nacional sobre la Desaparición de Personas*, CONADEP) to collect testimonies about the human rights violations. This was incorporated within the 'Never Again' report, which had an enormous public impact. The following September, the commission presented nearly 9,000 such cases to the president and documented the disappearance and probable deaths at the hands of the military regime of about 11,000 people, very few of whom were likely to have been cadres of the guerrilla movements. Yet CONADEP was not primarily concerned with themes that later became associated with TCs, such as truth-telling or reconciliation. Rather it was established largely to help make a case for prosecutions, and it identified 1,500 cases where there seemed to be sufficient evidence to indict military leaders. It was, therefore a quasi-legal tool.

The prosecution subsequently focused on just over 700 cases of murder, kidnapping and abuse involving those responsible at high levels. This paved the way to the opening of the Trial of the Juntas, which began in April 1985 and culminated in significant prison sentences for three generals and two admirals. However, the opening of the trials precipitated a reaction which was also of relevance to the subsequent evolution of TJ and schools of thought within it. For the prosecutions led to intense opposition by the military and other sympathisers of the dictatorship and threats to destabilise the new regime. This brought about the so-called Full Stop Law of 1986, which limited the possibility of further indictments, followed by the Law of Due Obedience of 1987, which halted most of the remaining trials. Finally, between 1989 and 1990, President Carlos Menem pardoned those who had been sentenced or court-martialled. Many in social movements demanding the end of impunity, and others who regarded trials as of central importance in bringing about accountability, saw this as a negation of justice and felt that their views no longer had influence on the transition. But another important strand of opinion in the emerging TJ field believed that such compromises were necessary and that pragmatism in the face of power realities was essential for successful transitions.

Two other highly significant changes of regime contained similar tensions but also reflected a further evolution within TJ. In neighbouring Chile in 1973, General Augusto Pinochet had carried out a violent coup against the democratically elected socialist government of Salvador Allende, which was followed by torture, mass imprisonments, disappearances and forced exiles. He had then instituted a highly repressive regime until he was finally replaced by a democratically elected government in 1990. However, this was markedly constrained by the enduring power of Pinochet himself, partly because twelve years earlier, in the aftermath of the most extreme period of brutality, he had passed a decree to ensure that agents of his state could never be tried for their human rights violations. There were protests against this amnesty at the end of the dictatorship, but Pinochet insisted on its maintenance and retained such extensive powers over the new regime that it feared destabilisation or even a new coup if there was any attempt to curtail his power or to undertake trials or purges.

Under these conflicting pressures, the transition regime established a National Commission on Truth and Reconciliation, known as the Rettig Commission, which subsequently reported that agents of the state had carried out the overwhelming majority of human rights violations and that the judiciary had been complicit in these crimes. But this TC differed from the one in Argentina, since it had no powers to indict the past perpetrators of human rights violations. Instead it recommended forms of commemoration of the 'disappeared', those executed for political reasons or tortured to death, and envisaged other attempts to bring about reconciliation, with material and welfare reparations. This was an important step in abandoning an insistence on judicial processes as the only legitimate approach to bring about accountability for past human rights violations. The incorporation of non-legal approaches inevitably shifted the emphasis in the emerging idea of TJ. Yet developments in Argentina and Chile, which stemmed largely from recognition of the continuing power of the former regimes, also demonstrated the fact that TJ practices would be influenced by pragmatism as well as normative ideals. Many of the underlying assumptions in the ideas and practices of what now became mainstream TJ were also shaped by the political orthodoxy of the era.

With the collapse of communism in the Soviet Union and Eastern Europe between 1989 and 1991, the West was now dominant and promoted a liberal ideological framework. Certainly, there were important differences within this outlook, particularly between advocates of a welfare state and those who favoured minimal regulation of the market, but the mainstream consensus favoured elections, multi-party political systems, the rule of law and capitalist economies. Dictatorships, whether of the right or the left, were condemned, and there was an implicit assumption that the universal road to peace and prosperity was through liberal democracy. The transitions from repressive states in Latin America thus took place in this wider context of epochal change, which shaped the development of TJ as a concept and practice.

Some of the important international conferences in which the new doctrine emerged constituted a microcosm of broader international processes. These reflected the way in which a notion of transition from 'dictatorship' to 'democracy' replaced and precluded other possible types of transition – particularly those of transition to socialism, modernisation or development (Arthur 2009: 337–43). The dominant assumption was now that the only relevant type of transition was one that set a given country on a path towards liberal democracy. This influenced the way in which those who helped to devise the conventional notion of TJ viewed the situations in Argentina and Chile, where attempts were simultaneously made to induce elements within the former regime to make their peace with a new order while satisfying their opponents and victims and survivors that a fundamental change was taking place. It was in this context that non-judicial processes, and particularly TCs, became increasingly prominent within TJ. However, these achieved their subsequent status primarily because of the importance of the Truth and Reconciliation Commission within the momentous transition in South Africa.

The ending of the Cold War, the release of Nelson Mandela from jail in 1990, and prolonged negotiations in a climate of continuing violence culminated in the first democratic elections in South Africa in April 1994, which formally ended apartheid. This was widely viewed as an event of major historical importance for the world as a whole, as well as for South Africa, both because apartheid was an outrage and because most observers had believed that it would survive much longer and would eventually be brought down only by a violent revolution. That the transition to black majority rule took place largely through a negotiated transfer of power was therefore remarkable, and the fact that the Truth and Reconciliation Commission was seen to play a pivotal role in this process meant that it acquired international prominence. Many criticisms may be made both of the limitations in the transfer of power and of the commission itself, some of which will be discussed later, but here we are focusing on its role in the development of TJ.

In many respects, South Africa fitted the framework of transition from dictatorship to liberal democracy. It was also conditioned by some similar constraints to those in Argentina and Chile, for the repressive agents of the apartheid state, particularly in the security sector, made it quite clear that any attempt to institute criminal trials would jeopardise the possibility of establishing a democratic system based on majority rule. Since it was equally unthinkable for the African National Congress (ANC) to countenance the blanket amnesty sought by the security sector, the initiative to establish the Truth and Reconciliation Commission was devised as an alternative that might reconcile these contradictory positions. But it transcended the conditions of its birth. This was partly because it was far more extensive in terms of personnel, research and range of activity than previous TCs, but still more because Nelson Mandela accorded it a central role in the project to build a 'rainbow nation'. Various features of the commission contributed to this aspiration, including the fact that it was led by Archbishop Desmond Tutu. His emphasis on forgiveness, accompanied by live television broadcasts of testimonies from survivors of repressive state brutality, communicated a compelling message of peace and reconciliation.

The Truth and Reconciliation Commission was therefore pivotal in enhancing the credibility and status of TJ – particularly internationally. For it seemed to be far more elevated in ethical terms than a mere compromise between the ANC and the current holders of power. Many saw it, and TCs more generally, as offering an alternative form of justice. TCs were held to be a better way of contending with the past than trials and retribution, since they involve alternative methods of truth-seeking and a partial move away from a focus on individual accountability to a more communitarian notion. As Ruti Teitel has suggested, this emphasis on truth and reconciliation also incorporated much of its normative discourse from other fields, such as ethics, medicine and theology. This meant that the relevant actors changed from the judicial and political spheres to those with moral authority, including churches, NGOs and human rights groups (Teitel 2003: 77–84). Because apartheid had appeared so likely to lead to a violent conflagration, and the Truth and Reconciliation Commission was so visible in the predominantly peaceful transfer of power, South Africa also played a particularly significant part in helping to turn TJ into a key component in international peacebuilding. To appreciate the significance of this, it is necessary to recall a further feature of the post-Cold War era.

While the main peacekeeping role for the UN had been relatively non-interventionist during the Cold War years, there was now a new confidence in the possibility of reconstructing states so as to overcome any propensity to internal violence. Following civil wars and, in some cases, external military intervention, the primary policy prescription was that the road to peace was through the construction of liberal democratic institutions and market economies. In 1992, in *An Agenda for Peace*, the then Secretary-General of the UN, Boutros Boutros-Ghali, inaugurated the new doctrine of externally driven peacebuilding as a means of ensuring stabilisation in countries emerging from violence. TJ soon became one of the tools of this new practice, and this was made explicit in two subsequent reports by the UN Secretary-General (UN 2004, 2011).

Ruti Teitel termed this as Phase III TJ, in which it was now applied to a situation of 'political fragmentation, weak states, small wars and steady conflict' (Teitel 2003: 90). The main ideological basis for TJ as part of the package of peacebuilding measures was very similar to that underpinning its perceived role in the transition from dictatorship to democracy (Sharp 2015), but it now also became one of the methods through which governments, the UN, international agencies and NGOs sought to reconstruct the systems of relatively poor countries. This reinforced some trends that were already present within TJ, such as the growth of international 'expertise' at the expense of voices from the areas of conflict. Critical analysts have therefore viewed this third phase of TJ, which also coincided with the era of 9/11 and the inauguration of the ICC, as a period in which the field became anchored in the Global North (Nesiah 2016: 10).

From the start, there had been an incipient professionalism in the circles that were developing the idea of TJ. As time went on, some key individuals became increasingly convinced that they were now acquiring expertise through analysis and experience. For example, the 1988 Aspen Institute conference was the first meeting that sought to clarify and solidify a conceptual framework for the emerging field. At this stage, one of its participants, José Zalaquett, had been quite tentative about what had been learned, stressing that no one yet had clear answers. Subsequently, he was appointed as a member of the Rettig Commission in Chile. Four years later, when participating in discussions at a conference in post-apartheid South Africa, he was more confident and concluded that a pool of world experiences was contributing to an understanding about justice in the process of transition (Arthur 2009: 323–4). At this stage, TJ was still comparatively experimental, but its enlargement of focus and prominence through peacebuilding played a crucial role in the development of professionalism, which simultaneously led to a tendency to regard it as a standardised package of mechanisms.

This process was evident in the evolution of some of the major international NGOs in the field (Subotić 2012), notably the International Center for Transitional Justice in New York, the most prominent body. This was founded in 2001 by human rights activists inspired by the South African example and began its work by promoting a broad set of TJ strategies for social healing, truth-seeking and reconciliation as possible alternatives to more legalistic approaches. Having started with four permanent staff members, by 2012 it employed more than 120 people, with five permanent regional offices and ongoing operations in more than thirty countries. It now also advocated a more 'packaged' approach, focusing on both trials and alternative justice strategies (ibid.: 117, 120). In theory, the UN opposed a 'tool-box' approach and favoured respecting local autonomy (UN 2004). However, the UN Office of the High Commissioner for Human Rights then produced a series of manuals from the TJ field, including best practice on a whole range of approaches. These were distributed to UN missions around the world, with guides, manuals and booklets, and the office also provided a roster of experts who could be called on to provide specific guidance on a TJ dilemma in a particular country (Subotić 2012: 116–17). Governments, the UN and major international NGOs in the fields of TJ and human rights played an increasingly dominant role in defining the content, approach and evaluation systems, and this advocacy network also ensured that the choice of post-conflict states was framed in terms of which model of TJ to adopt, rather than whether or not they wanted a system at all (ibid.: 118). This development has been parodied as a 'transitional justice' industry, composed of 'teams of experts, consultants, standardized software packages or data management, and a set of assumptions regarding how "to do memory" and why memory matters' (Theidon 2009: 296).

The expansion into peacebuilding also highlighted some dilemmas for TJ. The main zones of violent conflict tended to be in the Global South, but this raised questions about the extent to which the underlying assumptions of the 'experts' really fitted the prevailing conditions. Some now saw the problems in terms of the adaptability and flexibility of the initial ideas and how to tailor them to the demands of different kinds of societies. But, for others, the expansion of the field raised more fundamental questions about the whole way in which justice had been conceived within TJ, particularly in relation to socioeconomic justice. The involvement in peacebuilding also had a complex impact on the balance between legal and non-legal aspects of TJ. The second phase had seemed to be privileging TCs, but the extension into issues of peace and conflict in developing countries also led to a greater use of international judicial procedures. This was consolidated with the establishment of the ICC and also in a proliferation of hybrid types of court, which mixed both international and domestic processes. New international laws recognised an extended category of crimes and therefore also the range of past atrocities for which indictments might be possible. For example, the International Criminal Tribunal for the former Yugoslavia enabled the prosecution of sexual violence as a war crime, crime against humanity or genocide.

The global expansion also raised the question of whether TJ could be based exclusively on Western paradigms and power. The legal notion of individual criminal responsibility as a means of ensuring accountability was not a universal approach, for in many parts of the world traditional forms of justice had differing emphases. These were often based on collective notions about the needs of the community and the importance of reintegration rather than the ideas of guilt, responsibility and accountability. But nor did advocacy of non-legal approaches necessarily mean emancipation from a Northern and Western emphasis. For some of the dominant ethical and social-psychological discourse and underlying assumptions associated with TCs might also be regarded as culturally specific and alien to the approaches in many parts of the world. However, traditional justice practices also presented problems. For example, some indigenous systems advocated solutions that contradicted interna-tionally agreed norms or laws, for example with reference to gender. The extension of TJ into peacebuilding also brought gender dimensions into the field in quite different ways. For instance, in 2000, UN Security Council Resolution 1325 on Women, Peace and Security, which helped to raise awareness of the gender specificities in violent conflict, led to a greater consciousness of the particular types of brutality to which women were exposed both in repressive regimes and in situations of violence and conflict. Women have, of course, also been perpetrators of violence (Kaufman 2016), but Resolution 1325 demonstrated the major contributions that women could make in addressing past atrocities. All this generated new debates which were reflected in the evolution of TJ.

A further consequence of the global expansion of TJ was its contribution to a growing controversy about the extent to which the approach devised in any particular society genuinely reflected its autonomous wishes. While international peacebuilding may have reinforced a tendency towards professionalism and a 'tool-box' approach, it simultaneously stimulated demands for local ownership and control. Such protests also have relevance *within* societies, generating the criticism that attempts to implement systems of TJ have too often been formulated and implemented by governments and sectors of the elite. This has raised the question of whether processes that are ostensibly intended to help a society address past atrocities can do so effectively unless the methods and procedures are the result of a 'bottom-up' initiative. While such criticisms have developed partly because of accumulating experiences of weaknesses in TJ in practice, they have also drawn on earlier episodes in which social movements were squeezed out by the dominant approaches – as in the Argentinian case. TJ has thus become both more global in reach and more contested in theory and practice. The alternative approaches and critiques do not represent any single theoretical position or set of practical proposals, but together they have enriched the field while also partially emancipating it from its origins. Major aspects of TJ may remain part of what one influential critique described as a 'global project' (Nagy 2008), but there is now increasing diversity in assumptions, theoretical frameworks and practices.

This brief history has shown how TJ developed and became multifaceted. Its continued expansion has complicated the quest for an adequate way to conceptualise it in relation to theories of justice, the nature of transition, the interactions between the international, national and local, and the formal and informal methods through which the key concerns should be addressed. The next section considers some of these issues.

Defining and Conceptualising Transitional Justice

Defining TJ is a far more difficult task than it may seem. An initial problem is that even the term itself may mask many problems in the concept of 'transition'. Firstly, it might imply that the situations under discussion are fundamentally similar, but this is surely questionable. For example, can we really say that that the circumstances before and after both the genocide in Rwanda and the repressive dictatorship in Chile are in any way similar? Secondly, the notion of a transition might suggest that the most relevant major injustices began only under the former regime and will disappear under the new one. But, if the iniquities are deeply embedded in social and economic structures, a change in the political system might not make a very significant difference. Thirdly, by referring primarily to transitions in the Global South, is there an implicit message that deep injustices in the Global North, arising from the legacy of slavery and colonisation, have been overcome and that no form of TJ is applicable? These are important concerns which will permeate much of the discussion in the book and will be addressed explicitly in the final chapter. However, even if discussion of the problematic notion of transition is deferred until later, many other difficulties remain.

TJ is typically encapsulated in a succinct statement of overarching goals, followed by a set of mechanisms designed to realise these aspirations. There are considerable overlaps in the various formulations of the key goals, and many take a similar approach to that of Rachel Kerr and Eirin Mobekk, who suggest that TJ contributes to the restoration and maintenance of peace 'by establishing individual accountability, deterring future violations, establishing an historical record, promoting reconciliation and healing, giving victims a means of redress, removing perpetrators and supporting capacity-building and the rule of law' (Kerr and Mobekk 2007: 4). The International Center for Transitional Justice makes many similar points but highlights 'recognition of the dignity of individuals' as one of the overarching goals and adds, as complementary aims, other key objectives, such as 'making access to justice a reality for the most vulnerable in society in the aftermath of violations', 'ensuring that women and marginalized groups play an effective role in the pursuit of a just society', and 'establishing a basis to address the underlying causes of conflict and marginalization' (ICTJ 2017).

When translating the overarching goals into mechanisms, Kerr and Mobekk discuss the following: trials of various kinds (ad hoc international criminal tribunals, the International Criminal Court, 'internationalised' courts and domestic trials); TCs; and traditional informal justice mechanisms. Their approach is therefore primarily legal and institutional, while the approach of the International Center for Transitional Justice is again broader, for it adds 'reparations for human rights violations, through a variety of forms: individual, collective, material and symbolic', and 'reform of laws and institutions including the police, judiciary, military and military intelligence' (ICTJ 2017). However, each of the mechanisms is clearly designed to achieve certain goals to a greater extent than others, with the implication that there is a relationship between the *collective* impact of the mechanisms and the realisation of the goals. But the fact that most definitions embrace both goals and mechanisms raises a significant question: is it possible to understand TJ with reference to only one of them – goals or mechanisms – and, if so, which has priority?

There may be a temptation to suggest that TJ can be defined solely through a list of the most common mechanisms. However, this surely cannot be sufficient. We cannot define 'medicine' by providing a list of possible treatments or 'law' by naming all the courts, for some kind of generic description is necessary. It would therefore be puzzling if TJ could adequately be defined simply by an inventory of its most common mechanisms. Furthermore, this would not provide any help in answering the familiar question: what form(s) of TJ would be the most appropriate in a particular country or set of circumstances? It is not possible to assess this without some criteria for judgement, and this leads straight back to a discussion of goals, objectives and aspirations. Should TJ be assessed in terms of reinforcing law, or bringing about justice, or contributing to reconciliation, or creating an accurate historical record, or a combination of these and other goals? Thus an illustrative list of mechanisms, however long, cannot provide an adequate definition or conceptualisation of TJ. Is it possible to take the alternative approach and to identify it in terms of some underlying concept or objective(s)? There have been many attempts to do so.

Several normative goals are discussed in relation to TJ, including forgiveness and reconciliation, which, as already noted, played a particularly prominent part in the discourse of Desmond Tutu in the context of the South African Truth and Reconciliation Commission. Both forgiveness and reconciliation have been theorised, and significant attempts have been made to demonstrate their application in practice (Nussbaum 2016; Philpott 2012). Fruitful attempts have also been made to bring together a range of theories of quite different types in a transdisciplinary approach which seeks to create a platform reflecting the efforts to frame the subject conceptually (Buckley-Zistel et al. 2014). However, there are good reasons for taking justice in some form as the central goal of TJ, both because of the origins of the field and because this has received more attention in the debates than any other value or goal. But this begs the question: what is, or should be, the nature of justice in TJ?

Because the demand for accountability through trials was so central in second-generation TJ, as, for example, in Argentina, the dominant tendency in the early stages was to assume that criminal procedures, based on the rule of law and due processes, constituted justice (Turner 2016: 16–24).

This identification of justice with legality often continues, but its ascendancy was soon challenged, partly because, as we have seen, TJ quickly expanded into non-judicial fields, such as TCs and memorialisation. But this led to the danger that, without an adequate conceptualisation of justice, practice would become entirely dominant. As Christine Bell insisted, instead of allowing TJ to be regarded as a general field in which various approaches were seen as equally valid, there needed to be contestation over the different conceptions of justice, including that of law, and continuing negotiation between justice and the other goals of TJ. Otherwise it could become a cloak to cover and rationalise a set of diverse bargains in relation to the past (Bell 2009: 6, 26–7). Nor was this the only danger, for any suggestion that a judicial approach is unnecessary may sometimes help ruthless forces to use TJ measures in an entirely cynical and manipulative way. For example, following the recent civil war in South Sudan, which caused an estimated 50,000 deaths and the displacement of nearly 2 million civilians, nearly 70 per cent of respondents in a national survey on truth, justice and reconciliation supported the establishment of a war crimes court. However, the leaders of both the major groups that had committed the mass violations argued against trials in favour of a TC and amnesties. This was clearly to avoid accountability rather than because of any principled preference for non-legal approaches (Roach 2016: 1350–7). But, if legal approaches are required to play an important role in TJ, this brings us no nearer to an adequate conceptualisation of justice in a broader sense.

Ruti Teitel, who has been a major theorist in the field, initiated an important debate on this in her seminal book *Transitional Justice* (2000). Here she contended that TJ was not 'ordinary justice' because it was being implemented in extraordinary circumstances. Given this, she suggested that it would be inappropriate to expect a transitional regime to conform to the expectations of law and justice in a fully fledged democratic regime, which she defined in liberal terms. The system would necessarily reflect the characteristics of the transition, including the nature of the injustice that it was seeking to overcome, and it would inevitably be both backward- and forward-looking. While holding that there were some common features in situations of transition, Teitel insisted that each was specific, meaning that it was not possible to be prescriptive about the form of justice that would be devised and implemented.

Teitel's suggestion that the justice in TJ was of a distinctive kind, rather than 'ordinary', was extremely influential. For example, the editors of a collection of significant articles on TJ in 2012 cited it as 'a standard view' (Williams and Nagy 2012: 20). However, her claim that the justice in TJ was of a special kind has also been deeply controversial, provoking debate in both legal and non-legal circles. For example, some legal theorists have argued that the law in situations of transition did not differ fundamentally from problems encountered in stable liberal democracies (Posner and Vermeule 2003). Others have countered that there was a qualitative difference, as a transition demanded the establishment of wholly different norms and values from those of the abusive regime that it replaced, and these depended on a new legal system to underpin them (Gray 2010). More generally, though, Teitel's position has been contentious in regarding transitions as quite different from the previous 'bad' regime and the future 'good' one and for assuming that all roads should lead to liberal constitutionalism (Williams and Nagy 2012: 21).

Yet Teitel may also have provoked debate because pragmatism has been an integral part of her theoretical approach. She was prescriptive neither about the exact ways in which conventional legal principles might need to be adapted to transitional situations nor about the extent to which they might be buttressed by non-legal approaches. This also enabled her to accept the evolution of TJ towards peacebuilding and a world of constant change, seeking to incorporate later developments into her general approach. She has rejected any rigid notion of a trajectory and has accepted that TJ can take place in numerous forms, with both state and civil society actors, and she has also acknowledged that there can be major setbacks, with no inevitability about its progressive development (Teitel 2005, 2010). All this follows from the fluidity of her conceptualisation of the justice in TJ. Other theorists have rejected her view that the justice in TJ is distinctive and shaped by the contingent circumstances of each individual situation.

The philosopher Pablo de Greiff has been prominent in debates about TJ, having served as research director at the International Center for Transitional Justice from 2001 until 2014 and being appointed the Special Rapporteur on such issues at the UN in 2012. He has disputed Teitel's view of TJ as a special kind of justice, arguing that this defeats the purpose of establishing overarching normative categories to provide guidance in a variety of contexts (de Greiff 2012: 60). TJ, he maintains, follows the requirements of justice itself, but in special circumstances, and it refers to the set of measures to redress the legacies of massive human rights abuses. But, in his view, such measures as criminal prosecutions, truth-telling, reparations and institutional reform must be pursued together in a holistic way in order to attain partial goals, which are themselves stepping stones towards the final goals, which de Greiff holds to be democracy and reconciliation (ibid.: 40). TJ may be regarded as attempting to bring about justice only if it seeks all these goals simultaneously and does not accept trade-offs between them. And a successful implementation of TJ measures in the aftermath of an abusive regime is a precondition for further progress towards a fuller form of justice subsequently (ibid.: 65).

Yet de Greiff's own theorisation seems problematic. Firstly, while insisting that TJ is an application of the general principles of justice in particular circumstances, he does not elaborate on the nature of those principles (Murphy 2016: 21). Secondly, his position rests partly on claims about the impact or effectiveness of TJ. He thus suggests that victims and survivors are often sceptical about the measures that are implemented to address past atrocities in a partial and fragmented way. They would, he argues, be more likely to interpret them as constituting *justice* if they had good reason to view them as part of a multipronged effort to establish fundamental norms (de Greiff 2012: 38–9). But this is surely an empirical proposition rather than a theory of justice: for, even if victims and survivors *perceived* the result as more just, this is different from establishing that justice inheres only in the combination of these elements. Thirdly, de Greiff assumes that the effects of TJ measures are in harmony with one another and mutually reinforcing. But this is not always the case: for example, people may sometimes be less likely to engage in truth-telling if they fear that they may also be prosecuted, and both truth-telling and criminal prosecutions may sometimes reinforce polarisation. There may be irreconcilable tensions between elements of TJ, and an assumption of harmony between them is no substitute for understanding TJ in practice and examining the political dynamics associated with their often incompatible goals (Leebaw 2008: 117).

Many others have entered into these debates. For example, Colleen Murphy has recently sought to identify the distinctiveness of TJ by comparing it with other forms of justice that are often discussed in the context of transitions (Murphy 2016, 2017). TJ, she argues, is not reducible to any of these, and, in any case, they all fail to appreciate the special significance of transitions in general or the specific context of each case. The general feature of transitional societies, according to Murphy, is characterised by two features arising from the legacy of the abusive regime. Firstly, at the beginning of the transition, the relationships between citizens and officials are based on the unequal status of certain individuals or groups, and there is a history of collective and political wrongdoing being normalised. In this situation certain groups have been targeted for human rights abuses, and such targeting becomes a basic fact of life. Secondly, there is serious existential uncertainty, in which the future political trajectory of a community is deeply unclear. The core moral question, given these special circumstances, is thus how to pursue social transformation in a just way that distinguishes transitional societies from more stable ones. Murphy concludes that there is a fundamental normative framework by which the justice of TJ may be judged, but that this cannot determine the exact set of measures that should be implemented in any given situation. However, like de Greiff, she maintains that these should be pursued holistically and co-ordinated so as to be mutually reinforcing and complementary.

Although this argument is philosophically sophisticated, the theory is deliberately very general and is also an attempt to transcend divisions between the more conventional approaches to the field and more critical ones. While Murphy certainly seeks to address structural dimensions of inequality, these have been the primary emphasis of more radical conceptions of TJ. In a brief early intervention of this kind, Mahmood Mamdani argued that there needed to be a reorientation of approach, from a focus on individual perpetrators and victims to one in which social justice demands took priority (Mamdani 1996). However, it was Rama Mani, in her ground-breaking book *Beyond Retribution: Justice in the Shadow of War* (2002), who perhaps initiated a critical tradition that highlighted the socioeconomic dimensions of injustice.

Mani sought to apply multiple theories of justice by considering their application in the context of developing countries and peacebuilding. Following Aristotle's categorisation, she recognised three different concepts that were relevant to post-conflict societies. The first was legal justice – effectively non-arbitrary and 'fair' processes through the 'rule of law'. Secondly, 'rectificatory' justice was a system through which the abuses of the previous regime are addressed. Thirdly, there were issues of distributive justice, particularly in relation to the realm of socioeconomic, political and cultural inequalities. However, Mani argued that these had never been integrated in theoretical terms and, when considered separately, little attention had been paid in practice to low-income developing countries, although these were the regions in which violent conflict was particularly

acute and prevalent. Far too much attention had been paid
to 'rectificatory' justice and comparatively little to distributional issues.

In particular, none of the various approaches to inequality
had been adequate, and the fall of communism had
strengthened the trend towards justifying rather than diminishing distributive inequalities. While the idea of 'basic
needs', including food, water, shelter and clothing, had been
advocated in relation to measurements of absolute poverty
in developing countries since the 1970s, they, together with
social rights and equality, had been ignored in addressing
distributive injustice in low-income post-conflict countries
(Mani 2002: 38–46). Yet structural inequality tended to
be fundamental in causing the initial conflict, and such
distributional questions needed to be central in TJ. While
showing the philosophical shortcomings of the ways in
which all three aspects of the Aristotelian concepts had
been elaborated, Mani highlighted the lamentable ways in
which TJ had been implemented in developing countries
and illustrated these through several cases, including Haiti,
El Salvador, Guatemala, Rwanda and South Africa (ibid.:
128–47). Drawing together both her theoretical insights
and her conclusions about policy application, she sought
to devise a new and more integrated approach, which she
termed 'reparative justice', that would be less Western
dominated, enriched through a variety of cultural inputs and
philosophical traditions, and capable of achieving inclusion
in relatively poor countries in the aftermath of violent
conflict (ibid.: 178; Mani 2005).

Mani's work was a trailblazer for more critical thinking
within the field, opening up new debates about development
and other conceptions of structural injustice that could and
should be incorporated into both the theory and practice
of TJ. Some have suggested that the concept needs to be
replaced, or at least supplemented, by that of 'transformative
justice'. The general aspiration behind this idea is that the
focus should be redirected from transition to transformation.
One proponent of this view proposed a reconceptualisation,

incorporating political, economic, psychosocial and legal dimensions, and sought to define a transformative model which included six principles and a set of elements through which they could be operationalised (Lambourne 2009). Yet, although the notion of 'transformative justice' implies an alternative to mainstream approaches in TJ, it has been defined and utilised in various ways, and the concept remains equally elusive. It will be revisited in the final chapter, while some of the critical insights associated with it will be discussed throughout the book. But, rather than exploring these further here, it is necessary to explain my own position in relation to the debates summarised above in the search for an underlying conceptual framework for TJ.

I am sceptical of the possibility of achieving any consensus on the concept of justice in general and hence also on one which might underpin TJ. I take it for granted that the nature of justice is contested and hold that this will inevitably also permeate discussions of TJ. Some ideas are influenced by liberal traditions, some by legal thought and categories and some by Marxist or socialist theories; some emphasise structural historical factors; and some draw on feminist and other critical ideas (Newman 2016: 14–32). These theoretical frameworks are embedded within distinct world outlooks, making it highly unlikely that any agreement will be reached. But, although such a quest is doomed to fail, this does not mean that a search for adequate theoretical understanding should be abandoned or that the contestation is unproductive.

A central proposition of Amartya Sen's major work *The Idea of Justice* (2009) is that there is no need for a single notion of justice in order to strive against injustice. His own claim, drawing on Western and non-Western theoretical traditions, is that there are obvious, flagrant and remediable injustices that require action, but that these can be recognised and addressed without agreement on a single transcendent conception of justice. Christine Bell also makes a key point in celebrating the fact that justice and all the other goals of TJ are contested and concludes that this offers an opportunity to engage with a deeper justice project in an attempt to transform power relationships at both local and international levels (Bell 2009: 26). Such ideas inform my approach, and this book assumes that a common view of justice in general, or within TJ in particular, is not necessary in order to address past abuses and atrocities, to strive to prevent their occurrence, or to identify mechanisms that might be effective in these respects. And, while accepting that several concepts of justice contain important insights, my own view is that the ultimate objective should also be to transform the political, economic and structural injustices that lie beneath the violations. The interaction between different ideas and experiences of both successes and failures in complex situations lead to learning, though not in any linear way. Finally, TJ can never be based on any certainty about outcomes.

In an important work in the 1990s, Martha Minow expressed this position eloquently in relation to the constant dilemma of achieving a balance between the extremes of vengeance and forgiveness (Minow 1998). Vengeance, she argued, could create perpetual bitterness and an ongoing cycle of violence, while forgiveness was a condition that some individuals might attain in certain circumstances but which could never be imposed on others. In her view, trials, truth commissions, amnesties and memorials were all elements in an attempt to find such a balance, but she resisted any notion of 'tidiness'. As she said, she did not want to imply that it was possible to wrap up these issues analytically or achieve a sense of completion, and no response could ever be adequate for the survivors or their relatives (ibid.: 4–5). She saw her work as 'a fractured meditation on the incompleteness and inadequacy of each possible response to collective atrocities' and 'a small effort to join in the resistance to forgetting'. It was 'an effort to speak even of the failures of speech and justice, truth-telling and reparation, remembering and education' and 'a missive to the next generation … in the fearful acknowledgement that we are not done with mass violence, nor expert in recovering from it' (ibid.: 5–6). This is a poignant testament to the necessity of contending with the past in full consciousness of the limited predictability about the results, and this book considers some of the theories and practices through which this has been attempted.

2

Mechanisms and Approaches

Introduction

While chapter 1 considered the evolution of TJ and debates about its conceptual foundations, this chapter considers some of its characteristic mechanisms. However, some preliminary clarification is necessary. Firstly, the term 'mechanism' is less than ideal, for it suggests something like a machine, which is recognisable and distinct, remains constant, and may be used in a variety of circumstances. This also has a technical connotation, which applies still more to another frequently used term – the 'tools' of TJ. By an association of ideas, both terms may encourage the misleading notion that the field consists of a set of techniques. In reality, such apparently concrete phenomena as trials, TCs or memorialisation may take highly diverse forms; they are also shaped by the environments in which they are situated and are understood in different ways in different societies and by the various strata within them. Nevertheless, the term 'mechanisms' is so widely used that I have followed it here, leavened with that of 'approaches', to include such notions as retributive and restorative justice as well as 'traditional informal justice systems'. Secondly, some mechanisms in TJ have been excluded: there is thus little reference to processes focused on institutional change, such as rule of law programmes or security sector reform. This exclusion is not because they lack relevance but because they raise many wider issues about institutions and their relationships with social and political structures, and in a relatively short book a balance between scope and depth is necessary. Some of the mechanisms that are included are considered at greater length than others because they are discussed less in later chapters. For example, symbolic reparations and traditional informal approaches are examined more fully here than trials and TCs, which are analysed in chapter 3. The aim is to explore the rationale of each mechanism and to discuss some of the debates about them.

Prosecutions and Trials

As we saw in the previous chapter, Phase II TJ really began with the idea of criminal prosecutions as the primary response to the mass atrocity crimes of the Latin American dictatorships, and many view them as an essential ingredient in any programme designed to end impunity, establish the rule of law, remove some key perpetrators and, perhaps, help to deter future violations. The tendency has been to focus on relatively few individuals rather than attempting to follow the large-scale prosecutions that took place after the Second World War in some newly liberated countries (Huyse 1995, 2013). At the beginning of the twenty-first century, there appeared to be a downturn in the use of domestic courts, but there was subsequently a revival in Central and Latin America, with trials and convictions, including of those at the highest political level. A new stage thus began with the ultimately abortive attempt to indict Pinochet in London in 1998, galvanising a shift that was already under way in Chile. Since then there have also been significant trials and prosecutions in Argentina, Uruguay, Peru and Guatemala.

Trials and punishment are often, though not always, expected and demanded by large sections of the population, and there is frequently dissatisfaction when these do not occur. The idea of judicial processes is based essentially on the paradigm of criminal law and suggests that the perpetrators of mass atrocities can be tried and, when found guilty, punished on the basis of individual responsibility for their actions. This notion is also closely tied to demands for an end to impunity: that is, that such procedures, culminating in appropriate sanctions after guilty verdicts, carry the unmistakable message that crimes of this kind will not be tolerated. Yet the notion of a criminal trial is beset by paradoxes in relation to mass atrocity crimes. First, it raises the question of 'proportionality'. Criminal law is based on the idea that the punishment is proportional to the crime, even though different systems may have diverse ideas about the nature of proportionality in relation to specific crimes. But is anything 'proportional' as a punishment for mass atrocities or, at the extreme, for genocide? Many have argued, in respect of the Holocaust, that even legal language is incongruous in relation to such unimaginable evil (Simpson 2007: 83–4). Of course, most mass atrocities are not on the scale of those determined by Nazi extermination policies, but the question remains whether legal processes and punishment are appropriate. A second concern is the relationship between the attribution of individual criminal responsibility and collective behaviour. Individuals certainly either order or carry out torture, killings, disappearances and other forms of barbaric behaviour, but there are both practical and theoretical difficulties in the idea of individual criminal responsibility for such actions. The practical problems lie particularly in establishing the guilt of the high-level echelons and, above all, the political leadership, for it is normally difficult to find the incriminating evidence in orders or policy documents. But this means that the criminal law approach may lead to conviction and punishment of the 'small fry' and impunity for those who commanded them, as often happened in the early post-war period (Novick 1968: 158–70).

This danger of arbitrariness is related to theoretical problems in establishing individual responsibility for collective behaviour. It may make sense to regard many brutal leaders as personally responsible for the barbaric crimes that have taken place and even to suggest that these would not have occurred without them. But the violence also becomes entrenched through structures, bureaucracies and social norms, and fear among the population as a whole, including many lower level perpetrators. All this calls into question the relationship between the idea of individual responsibility and forms of barbarism that become entrenched in social and political structures (Subotić 2011). Yet, if there is a general expectation that those who transgress laws should be punished in some way, it appears to follow that perpetrators of the most flagrant crimes should also face retribution through judicial processes. This leads to a third difficulty, for retribution implies guilt, and this has posed problems for TJ.

One difficulty is that prosecution normally requires guilt on the basis of a clear law, but this raises the question of *ex post facto* law – whether it can be justified to institute prosecutions for actions that were only retrospectively deemed to be criminal. This was a major area of discussion in relation to the Nuremberg and Tokyo trials after the Second World War, which held German and Japanese individuals responsible for crimes of aggression, war crimes and crimes against humanity, although the basis for the charges under existing law was rather dubious. Such debates have continued, but, as discussed later in this section, they were partially resolved with the development of international criminal law, particularly when the ICC put prosecutions for mass atrocity crimes on a firmer legal foundation (Darcy 2018). A second difficulty is that, in 'rule of law' systems, guilt is supposed to be determined only through trials on the basis of evidence and due procedure and cannot be assumed in advance. However, since trials are advocated as a component in TJ partly in order to uphold the rule of law, an acquittal of someone who is widely viewed as guilty could be counter-productive, leading to alienation from legality as a means of retribution. On the other hand, a judgement of guilt without a clear evidential basis undermines the credibility of due process. These dangers illustrate a key paradox about trials for mass atrocities: their complex status in relation to law on the one hand and politics on the other.

Trials can satisfy popular demands for retribution and simultaneously uphold the creation or re-creation of a new legal order only if they normally lead to guilty verdicts. But this means that political factors are almost inevitably present in decisions about whom to indict. This does not mean that the judicial processes are comparable to 'show trials' in the Stalinist tradition, although of course they may be in particular circumstances, such as in the case of Saddam Hussein (Bell et al. 2007: 147–65). But it does suggest that they are to an extent 'political trials', in the sense that there are non-legal objectives in such use of judicial processes (Simpson 2007: 11–28). The aim is to indict those with relatively high profiles whose conviction is probable and whose punishment might have a major political impact, both in demonstrating the efficacy of legal processes and in satisfying the demand for retribution. Paradoxically, though, these objectives may be realised effectively only if the trials are generally *perceived* as being wholly contained within the legal sphere and not at all 'political'.

While there has been frequent use of criminal trials within domestic jurisdictions, there has also been a development of a network of international criminal justice through ad hoc international tribunals and courts; in so-called hybrid courts in which there have been various combinations of international and domestic involvement; in regional spheres, of which the Inter-American Human Rights System has been the most significant; and, finally, through the ICC since its establishment in 2002.[1] When considering this network, the differences between the power and wealth of states is of particular relevance, for, in general, international involvement in judicial processes and trials has operated in poorer and weaker countries or, as in the case of ex-Yugoslavia, with the International Criminal Tribunal for

[1] The idea of referring to all these as bodies as elements of a network of 'international justice' is taken from Kersten (2018).

the former Yugoslavia, in situations where external forces were involved in a military intervention. Here, and still more with the International Criminal Tribunal for Rwanda, it was hoped that such bodies could play a peacebuilding role in compensation for the lack of effective intervention to prevent the genocide. Subsequently, though, an additional concern was that the new Tutsi-dominated regime would not carry out fair trials against the most serious perpetrators, so there was a complete separation between the domestic system, in which the informal traditional system of *gacaca* courts[2] dealt with the overwhelming majority of cases, and the International Tribunal, which handled those accused of having a greater responsibility for planning the genocide. A further consideration was the lack of human and material resources to initiate prosecutions and trials, and this was also an important rationale in the hybrid Special Court for Sierra Leone, where both funding and leading personnel were provided largely by external forces. However, international forces also had their own priorities and sometimes their own 'agendas', which could lead to major tensions with national governments. This was particularly the case with regard to Cambodia, where a hybrid court to investigate culpability in relation to the genocide of 1975–9 was able to begin work only in 2006, after numerous delays and disputes. Some of the particular problems in relation to the tensions between external and internal priorities over judicial and other matters in various countries will be considered in later chapters, but I now turn to a more general issue about international criminal justice.

A fundamental assumption of TJ has been that it is rooted in a universal norm that mass atrocities are wholly unacceptable and must be proscribed through international and domestic legal processes. This idea was, as already

---

[2] The *gacaca* court system was an adaptation of a traditional system in which communities at local level elected judges to hear the trials of suspects below the level of planning the genocide.

argued, important in encouraging prosecutions for atrocities committed by the dictatorships in the 1980s in Latin America (Sikkink 2011: 64–7, 98–109). Subsequently, the failures to prevent ethnic cleansing and genocide in Rwanda and Bosnia and Herzegovina led to further shifts in the international framework, with the International Criminal Tribunal for Rwanda and that for the former Yugoslavia empowered by the Security Council to prosecute the alleged perpetrators of mass atrocity crimes, raising the expectation that these would no longer be granted amnesties. Finally, the Rome Statute of the ICC specified an international responsibility to take action in cases of war crimes, crimes against humanity and genocide. Articles 7 and 8 of the Rome Statute also incorporated advances made by the International Criminal Tribunals for Rwanda and the former Yugoslavia regarding such crimes as mass rape and other forms of sexual violence as both crimes against humanity and war crimes. However, the network of international criminal justice as a whole, and the ICC in particular, did not constitute clear progress towards universality, for it also exacerbated structural inequality within the operation of international law.

The ICC reinforced the external constraints on what a state might do in addressing mass atrocities. It was not entirely a question of what a government (or even the majority of its population) might choose as the best way forward in addressing past atrocities, for international criminal law was setting a requirement that something must be done, at least in the case of egregious crimes. However, this was not a clear advance in the establishment of international norms and laws, for many of the most powerful states in the world either stayed wholly outside the ICC or have not ratified the treaty.[3] At the same time, the UN Security Council has power under the Rome Statute to refer cases

---

[3] China never signed the Rome Statute. The US became a signatory under President Clinton, but in 2002 President Bush withdrew the signature, and the US has now informed the UN that it no longer intends to ratify the treaty. Russia was

to the Court, thereby almost ensuring that action is taken, while blocking the possibility of any similar action against the dominant states. Prosecution of those perpetrating the most appalling mass atrocity crimes is certainly desirable, but the ICC system thus means both that action may be taken in particular cases without consideration of whether this is conducive to a successful transition and that there is overt inequality within the decision-making processes. While there is always a political element in the decision to use judicial procedures for mass atrocity crimes, the role of the Security Council in prosecutions and the overwhelming preponderance of African states among the cases and prosecutions exacerbate this tendency. This has created a crisis between Africa and the Court, which will be discussed in the next chapter.

Purges, Vetting and Lustration

Following a change of regime, there will inevitably be numerous people, particularly in the public sector, who worked for the former state and were closely involved in its practices. Many will continue to sympathise with it, opposing the values and policies of the transitional government and perhaps even threatening its rule. Purges, vetting and lustration are designed to counter these dangers.

At the end of the Second World War, purges took place across much of Europe to remove unwanted individuals from positions of responsibility. These processes may have been a political necessity at the time, and it is an oversimplification to condemn the whole system. However, there were certainly many injustices, and the process was often arbitrary, uneven and inequitable (Huyse 1995; Judt 2005). More generally, there are significant difficulties for any transition state in purges of this kind. It will not want to antagonise whole sectors of the population if its position

---

originally a signatory, but President Putin announced Russian withdrawal in November 2016.

is relatively fragile or there is a severe shortage of skilled personnel and resources. Furthermore, there are advantages for a new government when many of those who worked for the former regime continue to offer their experience and expertise, and it may also be helpful for social reconciliation if they demonstrably shift their allegiance. There has therefore been a broad consensus that the post-war purges did not provide a model for later generations of TJ. The terms 'vetting' and 'lustration' are used to define and guide practice towards policies now viewed as preferable.

Vetting is widely regarded as a means of assessing individuals' suitability for public employment based on assessments of their integrity and professional conduct. In 2006 UN guidelines suggested that the purpose of vetting processes was to ensure that people with 'serious integrity deficits' were excluded from public employment in order to re-establish civic trust, relegitimise public institutions, and disable structures within which such individuals carried out serious abuses (cited in Horne 2017: 425). In contrast, purges target people for their membership in, or affiliation with, a group rather than on the basis of individual culpability, and without legal safeguards. They are also often seen to have different motivations: backward-looking, rather than forward-looking, and without the aims of establishing the rule of law, democratisation, reconciliation, trust or peace (ibid.: 426).

Etymologically, the term 'lustration' is derived from Roman times and refers to the process of purification. In the current era it has been put into practice primarily in post-communist countries in Central and Eastern Europe. However, there are disputes about the way that it should be defined. For example, it is often viewed simply as a regional form of vetting referring specifically to the laws and processes that were termed lustration in Eastern and Central Europe (Mayer-Rieckh and de Greiff 2007). But this definition has been criticised, both for failing to identify its distinctive characteristics and for implying that lustration cannot be applicable elsewhere. It was, for example, suggested in

Tunisia, Egypt and Libya in the immediate aftermath of the so-called Arab Spring (Horne 2017: 431–2).

Yet even though conceptual and definitional differentiation can be made between purges and vetting, with lustration regarded as a particular kind of vetting, there is no universal academic or practitioner acceptance of such distinctions. For example, the Transitional Justice Database Project (www.tjdbproject.com/#) puts purges, vetting and lustration into the same category, coding them all as 'lustration'. There are forceful conceptual critiques of this categorisation, and evaluation of the impact of the different approaches is also very problematic if they are lumped together (Bates et al. 2017; Horne 2017: 437–9).

The hope that the defects of earlier purges would not be repeated has certainly not been realised in full. The most notorious failure was not in any typical TJ situation but, rather, in Iraq after the US-led invasion in 2003. On the rationale that Saddam Hussein's regime had been based on the power of the Ba'ath Party, the American occupying forces introduced a deeply flawed de-Baathification process. This purged swathes of skilled military and civilian personnel and created new fissures and violent conflicts, producing devastating long-term effects that remain evident today. The whole programme was designed and pursued without reference to any modern experience, instead reaching back to de-Nazification, which had been flawed and unsuccessful (Sissons and Al-Saiedi 2013).

Vetting has been introduced in a wide range of contexts and in different ways, but it has not been applied to the whole public sector. For example, in El Salvador, following the twelve-year-long civil war between 1980 and 1992, vetting processes focused on the armed forces: 103 officers were identified, leading to some being sent abroad, some being retired from active duty, and some taking leave with pay and later retirement. In Bosnia and Herzegovina, following the break-up of Yugoslavia, vetting processes focused on law-enforcement personnel and judicial and prosecutorial positions. Employment was terminated for police officers who did not receive an appropriate certificate, while judges and prosecutors had to reapply for their own positions. The initiative in El Salvador has been regarded as reasonably successful (though, of course, its overall impact on the post-conflict situation in the country was very limited), but there have been some negative verdicts on the system introduced in Bosnia and Herzegovina, on the grounds that the procedures violated due process and reinforced the problems (Mayer-Rieckh and de Greiff 2007; Horne 2017: 439). More generally, it is unlikely that vetting often attains the high standards demanded by the UN guidelines.

Lustration initiatives in Central and Eastern Europe have varied considerably in timing and approach. In the Czech Republic, under a process that ran from 1991 until 2016, former Communist Party leaders, secret police officers, their collaborators and other 'wrongdoers' were excluded from posts in the state apparatus and barred from returning. By 2009 this had led to almost 473,398 lustration certificates being issued and over 10,325 positive lustration decisions. The Hungarian system, which began in 1994, gave high public officials tainted by the past an option of resigning or facing public revelation of their record. Although this was completed in 2005, there is still a form of public disclosure. In Poland, lustration started in 1997 and still continues, but in a quite different way from its original conception (David 2011: 7, 76; Horne 2017: 433–4). There are important questions about the effects of all three systems, how much difference the divergences between them made in practice, and whether the legal framework provides any real indication of the overall climate and impact.

One study sought to establish the results of different approaches in creating trust in the post-communist institutions and society (David 2011). This suggested that the Czech system, based on the notion of permanently 'tainted individuals', was exclusive; the Hungarian method, founded on the idea of exposure, was more inclusive; and the Polish process, which aspired to reconciliation, was built on confession. It concluded that the Czech system led to increased trust in government but, because it labelled people for life with a constant search for new suspect individuals, prevented any prospect of social trust. The Hungarian system was relatively unsuccessful because it was less effective than the Czech system in establishing trust in government and still inhibited social reconciliation. In contrast, the Polish reconciliatory system both promoted trust in government and simultaneously brought about greater social reconciliation (ibid.: 225–34). But these findings appear highly optimistic, and a later study, which also sought to establish the relationship between lustration and trust across thirteen Central and East European countries (including the Czech Republic, Hungary and Poland), was more sceptical. It suggested that lustration measures could improve trust in targeted social institutions, but that more generalised inter-personal trust might decrease as the scope and intensity of the abuses by the previous regime and the extent of complicity by citizens became known (Horne 2014: 248).

If lustration does undermine trust between individuals, this may be partly because it differs substantially from conventional vetting. It incorporates a notion of 'moral cleansing', implying something that goes well beyond a form of personnel reform. The range of institutions and sectors involved has also been far wider; the duration of the process is much longer; many more individuals are affected; and it involves truth-telling through voluntary confessions or forced public disclosures (Horne 2017: 432–4). Such features mean that the characteristics of the process, as defined in formal lustration laws and processes, do not always reveal what it can become in particular circumstances.

Poland is an extreme example of the way in which an initially limited approach has degenerated into something quite different. For lustration formed one element in a deteriorating political climate in which, over a long period, the pursuit of 'traitors', 'criminals' and those with a 'suspicious' past fuelled paranoia and a sense of victimhood. This culminated in the election to government in 2015 of the Law and Justice Party, which endorsed a revisionist and nationalist right-wing version of history, which transformed earlier 'heroes' of the post-communist transformation into villains. In January 2018 it also introduced a new law making it a criminal offence to suggest that Poles shared any responsibility for the Holocaust (although, after international protests, this was revised five months later so as to become a civil offence) (Tighe 2016; Peters 2016). In this context, lustration has assumed a quite different nature from how it was originally conceived, and the process is expected to last for at least another decade (Horne 2017: 434).

Lustration should not be condemned because of the form it can assume in a particular context. When controlled and limited by legal and political safeguards, it may be both justified and necessary. However, many concerns on both legal and moral grounds have been raised about it, including the use of unreliable and illegitimate secret police files to incriminate people and the tendency for the time period of the operation to be expanded, although the communist regimes collapsed so long ago. It therefore seems possible that some inherent characteristics in the conception of lustration may be closely related to failings when implemented in practice.

Yet there is one final important point to note about both vetting and lustration. This section has indicated weaknesses and negative aspects, but the alternative of foregoing any significant form of vetting also holds dangers. In Chile, for example, the post-Pinochet government failed for several years to attempt any change in the personnel of the security institutions or the judiciary, although both had upheld the dictatorship. This meant that a climate of impunity continued and that many of the most important levers of power remained beyond the control of the new regime. There may be problems in carrying out fair and effective vetting programmes, but the alternative may sometimes mean that a transition from injustice is jeopardised or even negated.

Amnesties

An amnesty is a formal decision by a government not to prosecute some of those who have allegedly committed a particular type of offence. It may be extended to everybody who could theoretically be prosecuted or to certain groups. Amnesties are perhaps the most contentious of all the mechanisms of TJ and are sometimes even regarded as incompatible with it. They are not really about ensuring justice and yet they may be a means of contending with the past or at least an ingredient in an overall policy designed to achieve this.

Proponents of TJ have generally condemned the idea of a blanket amnesty, as established at the time of the transition from the Franco dictatorship in Spain (for a defence of this approach, see Encarnación 2015). Yet amnesties have been a feature of almost all transitions, and in practice *de facto* amnesties of some kind are the obverse of a decision to restrict the number and range of prosecutions. However, this implies that amnesties come about for purely negative reasons, such as the practical need to restrict the number of trials, the shortage of experienced personnel in a new regime, or the fear of destabilisation. Certainly, many proponents of TJ remain sceptical about the advocacy of amnesties as a positive contribution on the grounds that they undermine the principle of accountability and could convince potential perpetrators that violent abuses may be carried out without negative consequences. In particular, from the perspective that holds criminal prosecutions as the default position for TJ, any suggestion that amnesties are normal and acceptable, rather than exceptional, may be regarded as negative (Laplante 2009a). This position is also underpinned by arguments suggesting that international criminal law, and particularly the ICC, has circumscribed the legal scope for both states and international authorities to offer amnesties for genocide, crimes against humanity and war crimes, although others argue that the Rome Statute may allow account to be taken through non-judicial mechanisms, such as TCs (Scharf 2004, cited in Kerr and Mobekk 2007: 65). At the other end of the spectrum are those who regard amnesties as a wholly legitimate and effective approach and argue in positive terms in favour of flexibility for governments in this regard (Snyder and Vinjamuri 2003–4: 6).

Attempts have been made to define a middle way between these positions. Louise Mallinder, for example, has sought to combine some principles of justice with awareness of political realities by suggesting that *conditional* amnesties may be important. These may be necessary in order to encourage combatants to disarm or dictators to transfer power, but they should take place in co-ordination with other parts of the transition process, including international courts and TCs. Amnesties, Mallinder argues, may be accepted if they fulfil certain conditions. Firstly, they must have democratic legitimacy, following widespread public consultation and endorsement. Secondly, they should represent a genuine desire to promote peace and reconciliation, rather than simply providing immunity for certain groups. Thirdly, they should be limited in scope so that, for example, those 'most responsible' could be excluded or certain crimes exempted, or, alternatively, the amnesty might apply only to members of particular organisations who participate in democratic and peaceful systems of political engagement. Fourthly, in exchange for receiving an amnesty, recipients must be required to reveal the truth or make public apologies or take other demonstrable actions such as community service and surrendering weapons (Mallinder 2007: 228–30; 2008).

This general approach sets out a way of contributing to the overall goals of TJ while avoiding the two extremes of legal absolutism, on the one hand, or simple *realpolitik*, on the other. It accepts that there are situations in which threatening to indict combatants or members of dictatorial regimes may simply lead to a continuation of violence, with further atrocities or mass human rights abuses. But, rather than simply offering impunity in return for peace, Mallinder's approach demonstrates ways in which conditional amnesties might provide incentives for some of those responsible for past atrocities to participate in the building or rebuilding of a new political order. However, this notion of how amnesties *could* contribute to TJ does not mean that this is how they have operated in practice, for pragmatic motives have generally predominated. Differing evaluations of their effectiveness will be considered in the next chapter.

Truth Commissions

Among the non-legal responses to mass atrocities, TCs have taken pride of place. Whereas trials are based primarily on individual criminal responsibility and retribution, TCs have been celebrated for their alleged ability to achieve a broader range of goals. Similarly, TCs have been viewed as more positive measures than vetting, security sector reform and amnesties. But a fundamental problem in any analysis of TCs is that their proponents have tended to exaggerate the multifaceted contribution that they might be expected to make. It has thus been argued that they provide broader approaches to justice than trials; are based on 'restorative justice', encouraging collective societal involvement in coming to terms with the past; give voice to the survivors of mass atrocities; offer a full account of history, giving birth to collective memories facilitating a rebuilding of the future; and encourage reconciliation on both individual and societal levels, contributing to 'healing'. A recent study of TCs has thus emphasised their malleability and capacity to channel contradictory beliefs into the same vehicle for social and political change (Rowen 2017: 149–63). However, by pouring so many alleged benefits into the single vessel of TCs, some of the proponents actually made it very easy for sceptics to dismiss the claims as overblown and untestable, as will be discussed in the next chapter. Yet it can be misleading even to treat them as one phenomenon, for they have been highly diverse in terms of procedures, purposes, resources and the degree to which they have sought to be genuinely embedded in civil society.

In his systematic study of the period between 1984 and late 2014, Onur Bakiner has provided a taxonomy of three generations of TCs, excluding unofficial ones or those in which politicians intervened to shape the results (Bakiner 2016: 24). The first-generation TCs were those established in Argentina (1983), Uganda (1986), Nepal (1990), Chile (1990) and Chad (1990) and also included earlier incomplete ones in Uganda (1974), Bolivia (1982) and Zimbabwe (1983). They were framed in relation to possible criminal proceedings and were limited to establishing the record on deaths and forced disappearances. They did not involve 'performative' aspects, such as hearings, and sought factual truth about crimes rather than historical explanations.

The second-generation TCs were established between the mid-1990s and the 2000s and addressed civil war and internal armed conflicts between government forces and insurgent groups in El Salvador (1992), Sri Lanka (1995), Haiti (1994), South Africa (1995), Guatemala (1997), Nigeria (1999), Peru (2001), Timor-Leste (2002), Sierra Leone (2002) and Liberia (2006). Of these, UN-backed peace accords set the scene for their initiation in Salvador, Guatemala, Timor-Leste and Liberia, and elsewhere incoming regimes, often under pressure from international and local NGOs, were responsible. All were established within a year of the transition, and some received significant foreign funding, with foreign activists and experts serving as commissioners or functionaries. These second-generation TCs had mandates granting a wider scope of investigation, taking in a broader set of violations. They also received much more publicity, with the South African Truth and Reconciliation Commission playing a key role in transforming the concept of TCs into an international and transnational project. However, they also assumed very different forms: while Guatemala's Commission for Historical Clarification and Peru's Truth and Reconciliation Commission undertook ambitious projects of rewriting their nations' histories and attempted to embrace previously excluded communities, South Africa sought to use its TRC for full nation-building.

A third generation of TCs, which began in the 2000s, involved considerable diversity. Many were in states that might be regarded as having consolidated political systems: Uruguay (2002), South Korea (2002), Panama (2001), Grenada (2001), Chile (2003), Paraguay (2004), Ecuador

(2007), Mauritius (2009), the Solomon Islands (2009), Brazil (2011) and Canada (2008). Morocco (2004) established a commission in 2004 under a monarchical authoritarian regime, and Colombia initiated a TC-like process well before the end of the civil war in 2016. Indonesia and Timor-Leste created a joint TC as part of a larger diplomatic move to strengthen bilateral relations. This third generation also established TCs as post-transitional institutions, with Panama and Grenada looking back to events that had taken place decades earlier, Mauritius examining the legacies of colonialism and slavery, and Canada addressing abusive and discriminatory schooling policies towards indigenous children. While first- and second-generation TCs were generally established by centrist or centre-left presidents or through peace accords, the third-generation ones incorporated a broader range of political actors and ideologies. Noting that several of the recent TCs have been established in consolidated political systems or non-transitioning authoritarian regimes to come to terms with the distant, rather than the recent, past, Bakiner suggests that they cannot be investigated with the same conceptual tools as those of the earlier TJ paradigm (Bakiner 2016: 27–43). But his taxonomy also calls into question any attempt to evaluate the generic impact of TCs.

Treating TCs as a single phenomenon, without agreement about an explicit set of criteria as to definition, can mean that a range of differing bodies are regarded as essentially similar. It can also lead to very different evaluations of their degree of success or failure, and it is more helpful to take a comparatively narrow minimum set of criteria (Wiebelhaus-Brahm 2009). Later in the book there will be some discussion of unofficial TCs and those in long-established political systems, but, at this stage, Bakiner's exclusion of them is accepted. Drawing from various existing definitions, I propose the following:

> Truth commissions are temporary bodies, established by, or with official sanction from, governments and/or international authorities to examine a pattern of atrocities or mass human

rights abuses during a specific period in a specific location in the past, perpetrated by state or non-state actors. They may use a variety of different procedures and approaches, but their essential tasks are to investigate, report and make recommendations.[4]

However, some commentators make presumptions about the goals of TCs that do not follow from a minimum definition, claiming that they seek to consolidate democracy or to promote justice, human rights, reconciliation or accountability when they do not all have such goals in their mandates. The inclusion of such goals and characteristics means that some TCs may be judged with unrealistic expectations to which many of them never aspired.

It is also possible for a particular TC to be highly successful in one respect but a failure in several others. For example, the Historical Clarification Commission in Guatemala had no power to subpoena, no search and seizure powers, could not hold public hearings, and was preceded by amnesty laws. It was also long disregarded by the government, so that initial judgements may have dismissed its significance. Yet its painstaking research led it to report that 200,000 people had been killed, 83 per cent of whom were Mayan, leading to the conclusion that the state had engaged in genocide against the Mayan community. Both the information and the analysis of the report were subsequently used in the 2013 trial and conviction of the former president, Efraín Ríos Montt (Kemp 2014: 147). The commission was an example of 'macro-history', which uncovered the structural dimensions of the mass atrocities and eventually paved the way for prosecutions. In contrast, the South African TRC

---

[4] This is a composite of definitions from various sources but is intended to be more open than some. In particular, it would allow the inclusion of international TCs (for example, those established by the UN) and also the possibility of one that dealt with atrocities that occurred in more than one country simultaneously or in border areas.

was clearly more successful in engaging a whole society and, at least initially, had a far greater impact. But, despite embracing a far more complex, multidimensional view of truth – factual/forensic, personal/narrative, social/dialogue and healing/restorative truth – its emphasis on subjective, micro-level forms meant that there was little structural analysis of apartheid and its key role as a fundamental cause of political violence (Chapman and Ball 2008: 144–50). The comparison also suggests that the impact of a TC cannot always be judged within the short term.

Yet a limited definition may also be a little too restrictive. For TCs are normally set up with some publicity and their reports are often (though not always) proclaimed with a fanfare. In most cases they are intended to make a contribution to addressing past atrocities that surpasses the formal terms of their mandate, and civil society groups often take their reports as a basis for making further demands. While it is therefore unreasonable to suggest that every TC should promote all the goals that may be attributed to them collectively, it would be reasonable to hope that each contributes to some goals that lie beyond its formal mandate. Their ability to do so is often impeded by a lack of resources, diminishing their degree of thoroughness and outreach. A further widespread problem, which is now more widely recognised, is that reliving painful experiences, particularly in statements and public testimony, may lead to retraumatisation. There are also important gender dimensions in this respect. It is notable, for example, in the testimonies to the South African commission that women were far more likely to discuss the experiences of their male relatives than their own position and were very reluctant to mention rape or other forms of sexual violence that they had themselves experienced (Democratic Progress Institute 2015: 60). Many TCs therefore seriously underestimated gendered and sexual dimensions of atrocities and abuses, although some later ones made important advances in this respect, as discussed in chapter 4.

The next chapter will review evidence about the effectiveness of TCs, but some preliminary points may be highlighted. Firstly, expectations about their possible impact should not be too elevated. For example, in some circumstances certain individuals might be helped psychologically and emotionally by the existence and procedures of a particular TC, moving along the spectrum from 'vengeance' towards 'forgiveness'. Desmond Tutu certainly hoped that the Truth and Reconciliation Commission would have this impact on individuals, but the empirical evidence on this is mixed. The results of one survey of 3,727 face-to-face interviews of a representative sample of the whole adult population in 2000–1 were encouraging in relation to some sectors, particularly among those of Asian origin and coloured South Africans. However, the findings in relation to the black majority provided less cause for optimism, suggesting that knowledge of the truth about apartheid had neither a positive nor a negative impact on attitudes towards reconciliation (Gibson 2004). The conclusions of some later research were more pessimistic, suggesting that the commission had not led to reconciliation (van der Merwe 2008: 41–2; Chapman 2008: 67–89). Individuals obviously differ in their psychological and emotional make-up, and it cannot be assumed that a particular social or political process or experience will affect them all in the same way. TCs may aspire to have an impact on social and political reconciliation, but any expectation that all individuals will want to 'forgive' may even be counter-productive (Madlingozi 2010: 215). Secondly, though, a sceptical view which holds that TCs prevent prosecutions without achieving historical truth is also too sweeping (Osiel 2000: 134–7).

Finally, despite their proliferation, it should not be presumed that TCs are a necessary or sufficient means of addressing the past in all situations and circumstances. Political authorities in many places, including Cambodia, Mozambique, Spain, Portugal and Northern Ireland, have not wanted to establish them, partly on the grounds that opening up the historical record in this way may reinforce divisions rather than helping to overcome them. In some cases, this might be an aspect of a wider refusal to address the past, but a TC is also a specific social and political construct, and it should not be assumed that it is a universally relevant contribution to moving forward.

Reparations and Redress

In December 2005 the UN General Assembly adopted a resolution setting out basic principles and guidelines on the right to a remedy and reparations for victims of mass atrocities (UN 2005). This defined victims as those who 'individually or collectively suffered harm, including physical or mental injury, emotional suffering, economic loss or substantial impairment of their fundamental rights', and added that the category could cover 'the immediate family or dependants of the direct victim and persons who have suffered harm in intervening to assist victims in distress or to prevent victimization' (ibid., Annex: para. V.8). The resolution provided a broad interpretation of reparations, inclusive of material and symbolic forms, with the provision of a wide range of services rather than simply direct cash transfers. The guidelines also specified that, wherever possible, the victim should be restored to the original situation before the violations took place, and this included 'return to one's place of residence, restoration of employment and return of property' (ibid.: para. IX.19).

In principle, reparations are perhaps the most victim-centred approach to transitional justice, for the benefits are aimed directly at victims and survivors (and society as a whole only indirectly), while the reverse is generally the case with the other mechanisms. Yet reparations – above all, in their material form – have generally been the most neglected mechanism of TJ. The most obvious reason for this has been the refusal of governments to devote sufficient resources to them, but the topic has also been particularly controversial and has resulted in sharp debates among advocates. A further issue has been that, once again, gender dimensions were absent from the early discussions and provisions, notably the 2005 UN Resolution. While most societies are discriminatory in relation to gender, repressive regimes tend to be still more patriarchal, and civil wars and violent conflict also have a particular impact on women. For example, although men are far more likely to die in the war itself, the mortality rate for women tends to be much higher once the conflict has officially ended (Ormhaug et al. 2009, cited in Democratic Progress Institute 2015: 18). There are also countless examples of sexual and gender-based violations being used as a weapon of war against both women and men, and this occurs in numerous other ways, including in camps for refugees and internally displaced people. Yet by 2005 reparations programmes around the world had taken almost no account of the difference that gender could make when conceptualising, designing or implementing reparations programmes (Rubio-Marín 2006: 23).

A trend subsequently developed to reverse this, both conceptually and in practice, and there was considerable discussion about the gender dimensions of reparations, together with some positive practical progress. Nevertheless, the Special Rapporteur on the Promotion of Truth, Justice, Reparation and Guarantees of Non-Recurrence noted in his October 2014 report that there were still too few instances where individuals had received reparations for serious gender-related violations through programmes with an inherent gender-sensitivity dimension (UN 2014a: paras. 69–73). More generally, most victims of gross violations still received no reparation, and there was an implementation gap 'of scandalous proportions'. This, he argued, did not affect only direct victims 'but ripples across generations and entire societies laden with legacies of mistrust, institutional weaknesses' and failing notions and practices of citizenship (ibid.: paras. 6 and 81).

It is widely accepted that reparations may be in both material and symbolic forms, and some general principles apply to both. However, there are also differences between them, and these will be considered separately.

(a) Material reparations

Apart from obvious problems about the *amount* of resources that should be devoted to reparations programmes, there are deeper divisions about their purposes and rationale.

The UN guidelines suggested that reparation should be proportional to the gravity of the violations and the harm suffered. This might have an intuitive appeal, but it also introduces an immediate problem of commensurability: in what way is any kind of material benefit a compensation for the death of relatives or a personal injury that has resulted from mass atrocities perpetrated by a brutal regime or in a civil war? The victim or survivor is an individual, but the suffering is the result of mass crimes. Under the abusive past, these individuals may have been subjected to the most abhorrent brutalisation and de-humanisation.

Material reparations may be intended to carry some kind of message about the present and future, but they can be a source of deep disappointment and alienation if set at a very low level or never made at all. This was the case in South Africa, where the Truth and Reconciliation Commission's proposal of a relatively low yearly payment for six years of approximately $2,700 was never adopted by the government, which eventually made a one-off payment of $4,000 to a narrow category of victims. Yet nor can payments normally be expected to be on the scale that a court might offer an individual for a death in a case in normal times: on this basis, for example, the cost of compensating the families of all those killed in the violent conflict in Peru would have exceeded the country's total national budget (de Greiff 2008: 456–7). This suggests a fundamental point: victims and survivors need to regard material payments as significant but not, in themselves, as offering full reparation. From a TJ perspective, other requirements have been proposed. Firstly, that the payment is made with open acknowledgement of the atrocities and that someone had responsibility for them. Secondly, the symbolic aspects of material reparations also include points about the future by indicating that, however the victims and survivors were treated in the past – and those who suffered the most from mass atrocities are often from marginalised and vulnerable communities – they are now regarded as full citizens with equal rights alongside all other members of the society. In principle, this could also contribute to promoting greater inclusiveness, bringing about higher levels of trust, both in the new institutions and across social cleavages (ibid.: 460–5). However, this is a theoretical rationale rather than a depiction of reality.

Discussions about reparations generally assume that the recipients should be the identifiable victims or survivors. Yet some argue instead that reparations should address structural and historical injustices or issues of development. This implies the need to address the underlying causes of mass atrocities and violence rather than to provide palliatives for victims and survivors. It has thus been suggested that, if reparations move money to a particular group without redistributing either wealth or power in such a way as to bring about any fundamental change, questions about amounts, and the case for receiving payment, will triumph over issues that might result in increased solidarity among a broader sector of the economically oppressed (Miller 2008: 284). Similarly, it has been argued that women are subjected to violations in civil wars because of the prevailing structures and attitudes of the relevant societies and that the task of reparations is to transform these conditions rather than to re-establish the previous situation (UN 2013, quoted in Walker 2016: 113).

As will be shown in the next chapter, evidence from survivors in the most affected communities in some very poor countries provides some support for this structural view. On the other hand, others argue equally strongly against it, claiming that the symbolic message communicated by material reparations is recognition and responsibility for past abuses, signalling inclusive and positive intentions about the future. Its credibility is therefore seen to depend upon the fact that this is conveyed to those who have suffered in particular ways as a result of those abuses. Such debates also take place in practical policy discussions. For example, the Truth and Reconciliation Commission in Peru found that most victims requested reparations that addressed their needs, which arose from inequitable social and economic conditions, and were not satisfied with a reparations model that simply gave them damages and returned them to the pre-war situation (Laplante 2008: 351–2; 2009b: 90, cited in Waldorf 2012: 178).

This led to some commission staff proposing collective reparations measures providing social services, infrastructure and economic development for the affected population. But they soon faced an intractable problem in defining categories of harm and causation, together with the danger of simultaneously losing sight of the specific recognition of victims and frustrating those who suffered from the same problems but were not included in the reparations programme. Such difficulties led to contradictory policies and recommendations, both within the commission and in the policies subsequently adopted by the state (Magarrell 2003: 93–5; Hayner 2010: 174, cited in Waldorf 2012: 178). Eventually, following a Comprehensive Reparations Plan approved in July 2005, two categories of victim were established, with both individual and collective beneficiaries, the latter reflecting an attempt to respond to the historic marginalisation of indigenous peasant populations in the Andes and the Amazon (Correa 2013: 6).[5]

Finally, the issue of restitution is one of the most complex and contentious areas of all. It implies settled legal systems and individual ownership, but this is normally far removed from reality in many situations, where conflict over land has often been the most fundamental source of violence in civil wars and ethnic cleansing. Once again the problems are

---

[5] However, the policy also included a new politically partisan provision, excluding 'members of subversive organizations' from being regarded as victims and receiving benefits, even if they had been tortured or suffered other serious crimes.

normally most acute in relation to peoples who have faced systematic discrimination, marginalisation and displacement. Difficulties in the notion of land restitution in these circumstances often involve the displacement of populations numerous times over centuries, particularly under colonialism; changes in forms of land ownership from customary and communal to individual; and transformation in farming methods so that, even if it were granted, restitution would be to land that is no longer productive. At the same time, the disputes over land which triggered the initial violence may remain as potentially explosive after a peace settlement as they were during a period of armed conflict or massacres. The dispossessed may often demand land restitution, but in reality far more extensive types of land reform and redistribution are also necessary.

This is illustrated in a particularly stark form in Colombia, where land is perhaps the most important issue in determining whether the peace settlement agreed in December 2016 will endure. Rural inequality was the central driver of the civil war, which was initiated by the Fuerzas Armadas Revolucionarias de Colombia (FARC) in 1964. But during this period of warfare, which lasted for over fifty years, the distribution of land ownership became still more unequal: in 2014, 1 per cent of the largest landholdings occupied 81 per cent of productive land (Guereña 2017). Furthermore, over 7 million people were forcibly displaced during the war, in which indigenous people and Afro-Colombians – particularly women in these communities – were the main victims (UNHCR 2017), while paramilitary groups, linked to landowners, were very often the beneficiaries. The agreements in the peace settlement fell well short of the demands initially made by FARC, and there is little reason for confidence that even these reforms will be implemented in practice. But the more general point is that the notion of restitution is highly problematic in such a situation and, like material reparations more generally, raises wider questions about development, inequality and historical injustice.

Overall, material reparations may in theory be the most victim-centred form of TJ, but they are also the greatest focus for dissatisfaction. This may be because of their absence or inadequacy, through false expectations about what may be given, or in the belief that they are directed to the wrong people. It may also be because they inevitably raise questions about the need for social and economic transformations that TJ itself cannot bring about.

(b) Symbolic reparations: memorialisation and apologies

Recognition of past atrocities through memorials and apologies has been a central element in TJ. In this respect, the influence of the memorialisation of the Holocaust has been particularly important, and the recollections of Simon Wiesenthal, a survivor and subsequent Nazi hunter, eloquently explain why this kind of public acknowledgement of the horrific experiences of the persecuted is so important. He describes how SS guards would torment the prisoners by playing on their apprehension that the wrongs they suffered would disappear, because they would seem to be exaggerations that no one would believe, and that the Nazis 'will be the ones to dictate the history of the Lagers [camps]' (quoted in Levi 1989: 11–12; Marrus 2007: 94).

The extermination camps were an extreme example of a more general phenomenon experienced by the victims and survivors of numerous other brutal regimes, particularly among those communities that have been subjected to long-term oppression and discrimination. This often leads to a conviction that, even if society as a whole is aware of their suffering, it is considered unimportant and will be forgotten. A long-standing brutal dictatorship will normally also seek to write its political opponents out of history – except as an entirely negative 'other'. Those who have dominated the state create their triumphalist monuments, name streets after their own heroes, and extol their military victories and values in museums. In addition to perpetrating atrocities, they attempt to silence numerous others through propaganda and public imagery. Acknowledging past suffering and victimisation in symbolic reparations that express a new set of values for the present and the future is therefore important.

Memorialisation may take a great many forms, among them authentic sites, such as the former locations of repression; symbolic sites, such as monuments commemorating victims, survivors and resisters; renamed streets and buildings; physical or virtual museums of history and memory; and such activities as reburials or vigils. Memorialisation construction has escalated enormously since the 1980s, often linked specifically to the wider goals of TJ, but it also raises some difficult questions. Imagery and historical narratives may be very persuasive, but what messages are conveyed, who are the target audiences, and who decides?

In the context of TJ, memorials may be a form of redress, but, once again, this involves identification of the primary victims. This may not be too problematic if a memorial is on the site of a massacre and the accompanying placard simply records the names of those who were killed, but there are far greater difficulties when a wide-ranging phenomenon is commemorated. For example, the Nazi genocide of European Jewry is a fact, but there can still be controversies about the way that it is memorialised. Thus, when Berlin established a 'Memorial to the Murdered Jews', some people were offended that there was no mention of others, such as Roma, homosexuals and people with disabilities, who were also systematically killed by the Nazis. Similarly, while the overwhelming majority of victims in the Rwandan genocide were Tutsis, there were also Hutu victims, but in 2008 the phrase 'genocide perpetrated against the Tutsis' was officially decreed, deliberately repressing the memory of Hutu suffering. Memorialisation is inevitably selective, and sometimes this is for conscious political purposes (Moore 2009).

On the assumption that there is agreement about the identity of the primary victims, a second question concerns the extent to which they are involved in the design and control of the form of memorial that is established. The South African Truth and Reconciliation Commission recognised the important point that symbolic reparations of this kind should be linked with endeavours to improve the everyday lives of victims and their communities by giving them a prominent role in designing and manufacturing the monuments (UN 2014b: para. 94). This recommendation was subsequently followed in Robben Island, where former political prisoners took a key role as guides for tourists. In Rwanda, however, a constitutional revision in August 2008 led to much greater state control over monuments and a reduction in local autonomy and variation (Dumas and Korman 2011). And, although a fundamental purpose of memorialisation is to empower victims and survivors, they often receive little feedback on decisions taken in their name and are left with a victim status rather than actively participating in establishing and controlling the memorial (UN 2014b: para. 97). A further crucial issue is the nature of the message that is promoted.

History and memorialisation have played a key role in the construction of national and ethnic myths, often with deeply negative effects. David Rieff has thus put forward the contentious argument that the price of remembering some historical grievances is too high, and that there are cases in which 'it is not the duty to remember but a duty to forget that should be honored' (Rieff 2016: 121). It is true that constantly reverting to bitter events of the past can impede any attempt to bring about peace, which is why partisan history is a potent weapon of many extreme nationalist forces. But it is equally dangerous to seek to erase historical memory, and the real question is therefore not *whether* to remember the past, but *how* to do so.

The value of memorials is clearly related to the kind of narrative about the past and conception of the future that they seek to promote. A symbolic message which suggests, explicitly or implicitly, that all evil lies in one ethnic group (the perpetrators) and all virtue in another (the victims) is hardly designed to bring about trust and possible eventual reconciliation. On the other hand, it may often be necessary to recall that it was the regime or particular political movement that was primarily responsible for atrocities and mass human rights abuses. Museums and other forms of memorialisation carry a heavy responsibility in attempting to steer their way through these contradictory pressures. Louis Bickford argues that, when done well, forms of memorialisation can succeed in this task by making an emotive appeal arising from the visitors' forced encounter with past atrocities, and simultaneously impelling them to address major questions about the present and future. At best they can be an element in a broader civic dialogue about the past, raising questions and debates about existential matters and compelling people to face the most difficult problems a nation can address about its past (Bickford 2014: 515). However, many memorials fall far short of such a standard. For example, in each part of Bosnia and Herzegovina, the local majority ethnic group has had a monopoly in deciding the form of memorialisation while other groups have been excluded from the purpose, leading to ethnically divided memorials that provide little or no space for alternative narratives (Impunity Watch 2013).

The Special Rapporteur on Culture for the UN has made several valuable recommendations as to how to maximise the possibilities of achieving positive goals, while also warning of the danger that memorialisation will be used to further particular agendas (UN 2014b: paras. 98–106). Those who have considered memorialisation as part of a wider movement for transformation rather than simply as a matter of redress and reparations have sought to prevent this. Impunity Watch, which operates on the basis of a 'bottom-up' approach, has identified a challenging set of principles of memorialisation, based on comparative research in Bosnia and Herzegovina, Burundi, Cambodia and South Africa (Impunity Watch 2013). These principles highlight the necessity to consider the root causes of violence, the nature of the conflict, the current social and political situation, and the enduring legacies, including structural violence. The report emphasises the need for attention to the diverse ways in which memory initiatives can contribute to the goals of political and institutional reform, addressing socioeconomic inequalities and demands for human rights. It also reveals much about the complex ways in which memorialisation can both empower and constrain, sometimes in paradoxical ways. For example, although the involvement of victims in former sites of repression in South Africa was widely regarded as positive, participation in them may sometimes have accentuated feelings of injustice and despair about the continuing post-apartheid socioeconomic inequalities. In contrast, in the Ixhil region of Guatemala, the lack of involvement and absence of representation of the history of their community in the national truth project drove the Q'eqchi' to challenge the dominant discourse in local memorialisation, helping to transform themselves from passive 'victims' to an active role as rights-claiming 'survivors'.

If memorialisation is to be effective, it should not be used in an instrumental manner. This means that international forces should facilitate, rather than dominate, the conception and realisation of the plans. The negative impact of international control of the processes has been particularly apparent in Bosnia and Herzegovina. One notorious example was when external actors regarded the reconstruction of the beautiful sixteenth-century Ottoman Old Bridge at Mostar as an important symbol of reconciliation across the lines of violence. However, it had little impact of this kind, partly because the rhetorical 'hype' resulted from a lack of understanding of the persisting nationalist sentiment in the locality. More damaging still was the internationally led attempt to construct a memorial at the notorious former Omarska camp in Bosnia and Herzegovina, for this may have helped to reinforce a victim–perpetrator dynamic that impeded progress in intercommunity relations (Sivac-Bryant 2015).[6] On the other hand, as long as it avoids instrumentalisation

---

[6] The Bosnian-Serb Omarska camp held around 6,000 Bosniak and Croat prisoners for about five months in appalling conditions in 1992.

of this kind, some form of external role can be necessary and helpful when local communities are locked into competing narratives of victimhood.

If memorialisation is to have a long-term impact, it is crucial that younger generations are involved so as to ensure that sites have contemporary as well as historical importance. For example, many young people in Cambodia who visited the state-run Tuol Sleng Genocide Museum at the former Khmer Rouge torture centre remained confused, but civil society initiatives directly targeting young people led to far greater intergenerational understanding, with young people mobilising all age groups. Museums, sites of conscience and education-focused NGOs may have the most potential for longevity, for more formal attempts to incorporate active reflections on the past into the formal school curriculum have generally been disappointing (Cole 2017). However, as a study in Guatemala has suggested, there are difficulties in judging the success of such projects. Here there was a campaign for inter-ethnic dialogue to foster social reconciliation and address racism. A central element was an interactive museum exposition called 'Why are we the way we are?', which invited people to reflect on their own lives while experiencing a multi-media depiction of the history and current state of inter-ethnic relations. The campaign was highly successful in terms of participation, for it reached 25 per cent of the local population and 40 per cent of school students in two of the three Guatemalan departments where the exposition was set up. But when attempts were made to judge the impact in terms of changing attitudes, it became clear that this was a highly complex task (Duggan 2010a). In fact, memorialisation highlights some of the complexities in the evaluation of TJ in general, which will be considered in the next chapter.

In many respects, apologies, as a form of symbolic reparations, are a subset of memorialisation, and, with varying degrees of sincerity, they too have been proliferating since the 1980s. They have sometimes been denigrated as a costless exercise that means little in the way of reparation, but this is too dismissive. In fact, victims and survivors often call for such action, and effective apologies clearly have a high symbolic value. Of course, in themselves they will do little to provide any kind of redress, but in conjunction with other forms of reparation and wider TJ measures they can have significance. Since they are normally public acts with media coverage and are scrutinised by civil society movements and other interested parties, they often symbolise an important step in the attempt to address the past. Much depends on the way in which the apology is delivered. For example, Japanese attempts to apologise for atrocities in Asia during the Second World War have been unsuccessful because they have been partial and coupled with other forms of behaviour (such as continuing prime ministerial visits to the Yasukuni Shrine, where war criminals are buried) that appear to contradict the words that are spoken. In contrast, Chancellor Willy Brandt's spontaneous and sincere act of kneeling to the Jewish victims of the Warsaw Ghetto during a state visit to Poland has been viewed as one of the most effective apologies in history.

There is widespread agreement about some of the key aspects in an effective apology, including acknowledgement of the wrong that has been committed, the harm that it has caused, an acceptance of responsibility and an expression of regret or remorse, coupled with a commitment to reparation and non-repetition (Marrus 2007: 79). Nor does this consist simply of a form of words, however appropriate and sensitive these may be, for it must include an element of dialogue. Whether this takes place through a physical presence in the territory where the acts were committed or in other ways, the speaker must communicate to the key target audience that the words spoken symbolise deeper meanings and commitments. All this has often been agreed in advance with survivors, their families and other representatives, and this very act of agreement may also have significance, for it implies some acceptance of equality between perpetrators and victims. The International Center for Transitional Justice has highlighted several successful cases and suggested their general characteristics.

Among the successes, it notes the journey in October 2014 of representatives of four Ecuadorian governmental ministries and the office of the attorney general, deep into the Amazonian forest, to apologise to the Sarayaku indigenous peoples for human rights violations committed there in 2003 and to give a pledge to honour the commitment to human rights in future (Carranza et al. 2015: 15). Another important apology was that in 2010 by the president of Sierra Leone to the women of the country for the brutalities that they had suffered during the armed conflict (ibid.: 8–9). This was coupled with the launch of a National Gender Plan, and in his apology the president specifically highlighted a commitment to remove long-standing inequalities in health, education and political representation and to strive for gender justice, equal rights and equal opportunities. Finally, the apology in 2012 by the Salvadorian president for the atrocities in El Mozote in December 1981, where the army killed 936 people and carried out a mass rape of women and girls, encompassed many of the key elements in a successful apology: it was agreed in advance by the victims or their representatives; it was public; it was at the place where the events had occurred; responsibility for the extrajudicial executions and other violations was acknowledged; it was held in the presence, and with the participation, of a considerable number of survivors and next of kin; the highest state authority (the president) and senior state officials took part; and it was broadcast and disseminated fully throughout the country (ibid.: 18).

In principle, then, memorialisation and apologies can contribute both to the process of reparation for victims and survivors and to wider social and political goals. Yet the current situation in El Salvador also illustrates their limitations unless accompanied by more fundamental changes. For the social and economic inequalities that triggered the original violence remain unresolved, and El Salvador is a very violent country, with an extremely high murder rate despite the civil war having formally ended in 1992 (Wade 2016). The potential importance of symbolic reparations should not be minimised, but nor should their independent impact be exaggerated.

Traditional Informal Justice

Traditional informal justice (sometimes also known as 'indigenous justice') is not, of course, a 'mechanism' of TJ, and the term itself suggests a view from the 'outside', primarily from the Global North. In fact, at least 80 per cent of disputes in fragile states may be settled through informal justice procedures rather than through formal legal systems (OECD 2007, cited in Allen and Macdonald 2013: 3). The increasing role of external forces in TJ in post-conflict situations in developing countries made it inevitable that theorists and practitioners would confront situations in which formal legal systems would coexist with a range of more traditional informal methods at local level and would need to grapple with the problems inherent in this kind of legal pluralism. However, particularly in the early 2000s, some advocates of TJ went further and viewed traditional informal justice methods as a potential solution to weaknesses in mainstream TJ arising from its tendency to promote universal approaches. Subsequently, however, there has been a reaction to an oversimplification and romanticisation of traditional informal justice.

The first difficulty in even discussing the advantages and disadvantages of such systems is that they are highly diverse, not only between countries and regions but within them. For example, there are numerous different systems within Papua New Guinea and across Indonesia (UNICEF 2009) and even within a small country such as Guatemala (Arriaza and Roht-Arriaza 2008). Nor are they static or even necessarily very traditional but, rather, subject to fluidity and mutation (Allen and Macdonald 2013: 18–21). It is therefore clearly misconceived to treat informal justice as a homogeneous category. There is no agreed definition, but the term is normally used to refer to systems where the resolution of disputes is by political, hereditary or spiritual authorities within a community, with the assumption that crimes and disputes affect the community as a whole and that the primary purpose is to maintain this and its cultural tradition, and where the informality lies particularly in the fact that it does not follow the procedures of formal law-based processes, such as written rules, or legal representation (Kerr and Mobekk 2007: 152–6; McAuliffe 2013a: 49–50).

The advantages of such systems are that they tend to be more accessible, rapid and affordable than distant courts, and the decisions are made by familiar elders or others who speak the local language. The objective is usually to maintain harmony and to promote reconciliation, bringing about closure for the community as a whole. A traditional justice system also tends to be more flexible than formal legal processes, adapting more easily to the particular circumstances of the case. Because it is familiar, it may also be expected to have more local legitimacy than a court in a distant capital, let alone abroad.

Certainly informal justice processes can sometimes be very helpful. For example, a degree of communal reconciliation through reintegration rituals for lower level ex-soldiers and perpetrators took place in Sierra Leone; in Timor-Leste, there have been more than 200 hearings for 1,376 perpetrators with up to 40, 000 people attending; and in Peru, Burundi and Afghanistan, traditional justice processes have also been partially effective and legitimate in addressing post-conflict justice (Allen and Macdonald 2013: 10, 12, 17). In Guatemala many local initiatives sharing Mayan belief systems may have been more successful in relation to community reintegration than the formal processes of TJ, although it is not clear that they have been applied to the tensions arising from the legacy of the armed conflict (Arriaza and Roht Ariaza 2008: 169).

Finally, there is the case of Rwanda, where, between 2001 and 2012, a modified form of an informal justice system, the *gacaca* courts, dealt with the overwhelming majority of cases related to the genocide. In a major study, Philip Clark is relatively sympathetic, stressing that the *gacaca* processed some 2 million cases and achieved a degree of coexistence in the most appalling circumstances (Clark 2010). However, others are far more critical, highlighting disregard of human rights, partiality, and a refusal to deal with the crimes of the victorious Tutsi-dominated Rwandan Patriotic Front against Hutus (Waldorf 2006; Human Rights Watch 2011). A forceful critique has also argued that, while represented as a form of restorative justice, in practice the *gacaca* reinforced the collective guilt of the Hutus and have actually tended to add to both ethnic and class tensions (Longman 2017). This example of Rwanda may demonstrate the more general problem that enthusiasm for traditional informal justice has sometimes led to an uncritical attitude that overlooks major weaknesses.

One reason was a belief that such systems had some advantages over Western forms of restorative justice. Certainly, TCs do not always resonate with traditional societies because they are often based on inappropriate models. The location of the commission in the capital and the promulgation of a formal, factual truth based on historical evidence are often inappropriate in a community following an oral tradition. It therefore seemed that indigenous practices would be more likely to bring about the kind of reconciliation emphasised in TJ. However, while the major purpose of most informal systems is indeed to bring about community reintegration, this does not mean that the whole emphasis is upon restorative justice rather than punishment and retribution. In Guatemala, for example, punishments for serious violations of community practices may include whipping with a tree switch and other physical discomforts, temporary or permanent banishment, or ostracism (Arriaza and Roht-Arriaza 2008: 169). In Northern Uganda punitive measures have always been common, and in many parts of Africa heinous crimes, such as witchcraft, have carried severe punishment (Allen and Macdonald 2013: 11–12). It is, in fact, probable that the distinction between Western and indigenous systems has been exaggerated and that both have included both restorative and retributive elements. Furthermore, people in indigenous communities who use informal justice systems do not always want to do so for serious crimes. In Timor-Leste, for example, while 69 per cent would use local justice methods for theft (and only 13 per cent the formal system), over 90 per cent regard the formal system as more appropriate for murder trials (McAuliffe 2013a: 72, citing Pigou 2004: 34).

A major problem is that traditional informal justice systems naturally reflect the power and status hierarchies of the communities in which they are based. Many of these are structured in deeply patriarchal and hierarchical ways. In Fiji, for example, these are so marked that many women and young people view appeals to 'tradition' as ways of maintaining an existing status quo at their expense (UNICEF 2009). In some countries, traditional customs for dealing with violence against women, including rape, are incompatible with all international agreements and even the laws of the country. Thus, in one case in Timor-Leste, the village council 'punished' a rapist by chaining him to the victim's bed. As Kerr and Mobekk note, this surely meant that she was punished more severely than the perpetrator (2007: 159). A further problem is that the informal systems may have utility only within a relatively small and homogeneous area of a country and will not be accepted for intercommunity disputes. Some central governments may not want to recognise traditional justice methods, but elsewhere it may be very convenient for them to do so, for, by encouraging local-level informal systems, governments may sometimes seek to divert attention from themselves. This appears to have been the case both in Uganda (Allen and Macdonald 2013: 10) and in Timor-Leste, where localisation of TJ processes may imply that the problem is between different groups rather than between the state and its citizens (ibid., citing Drexler 2009: 50).

Traditional informal justice systems may often be effective and carry local legitimacy, and they will clearly continue to coexist with state legal systems. But this is quite different from suggesting that they are always preferable. Even when they are embedded locally, it cannot be assumed that this is invariably because they are favoured by the communities that use them. Sometimes it may be that local experience of a formal legal system has been one of corruption or prohibitive cost, or simply that it is too distant. However, national reforms could overcome or mitigate these problems, and, as already noted, there is often already a preference for dealing with really serious crimes at state level. Given the association between mainstream TJ and liberal thought, it would be paradoxical to adopt a universal preference for traditional systems, even in cases where they flagrantly transgress international human rights and gender equality norms.

Yet there are also cases of mutual benefit through interaction and accommodation between formal and informal systems. In Sierra Leone and Timor-Leste, state law has recognised and sanctioned traditional justice in some spheres (Allen and Macdonald 2013: 7). Sometimes indigenous systems have also been used to challenge traditional values and practices. For example, women have led local truth-seeking projects in Sierra Leone and have had greater involvement in Rwandan *gacaca* courts than was traditionally allowed. There have also been active women's courts in Guatemala and Colombia (McAuliffe 2013a: 84; Allen and Macdonald 2013: 15). But there is little evidence that informal systems are able to deal with mass atrocity crimes. Certainly, they tend to be more receptive than formal criminal approaches to an understanding of 'grey areas', such as the inappropriateness of hard-and-fast distinctions between perpetrators and victims – for example, in the case of child soldiers (Allen and Macdonald 2013: 13). But, thus far, there is no formula for integrating traditional and formal systems, and it seems more sensible to consider their relationship on a case-by-case base than to romanticise informal justice as a solution to the problems of TJ.

Concluding Remarks

This chapter has considered a wide range of mechanisms and approaches to TJ. What emerges is inevitably variegated and multidimensional, for each has both strengths and weaknesses. For example, criminal trials ensure that some key perpetrators of mass atrocities are held to account, ending the climate of impunity and upholding the idea that the transition society is built upon the rule of law. In some circumstances, trials of major figures may also have a cathartic effect, even if they do not lead to a conviction. Thus, while the attempt to convict General Pinochet was ultimately abortive, it was the catalyst for further important changes. It galvanised more open discussion of the past in Chile and facilitated a gradual dismantling of the blanket amnesty so that other perpetrators were brought to trial. Yet the use of the legal system in TJ also has some major limitations. Trials may be very remote from the lives of the primary victims of past abuses, both because they are held far away in distant capitals or abroad and because the discourse and underlying assumptions of criminal procedures are quite different from those of many poor people in rural societies. Furthermore, prosecutions of a relatively small number of individuals do not address the root causes of abuses or tackle the structural features of a society in which those abuses may be embedded.

Analysis of each of the other mechanisms reveals a similar range of merits and demerits, as exemplified in the discussion of reparations. These are the most victim-centred of all the forms of TJ and can carry a crucial message that the transition will usher in a new era quite different from its predecessor. This may be of particular importance to the most marginal and vulnerable communities. Yet redress through reparations is also one of the most problematic mechanisms. The prospect of material benefits may raise expectations about the relief of long-term deprivation, leading to deep disillusionment when they are not delivered or are offered only at a very low level. Sometimes new conflicts may even be unleashed about which section of the population has the strongest claim on any available payments. Symbolic reparations also have both strengths and weaknesses. When the affected communities are fully involved in devising and establishing memorials or participate fully in ensuring that any apologies are appropriate, the results may be significant. On the other hand, when governments or international actors seek to use symbolic reparations in an instrumental way, they are likely to have little impact and may be counter-productive.

A further important point highlighted in the chapter is that the effects of each mechanism are context-dependent. TJ initiatives are implemented from a variety of motives and with multiple objectives. This is perhaps the most obvious in the case of TCs, where the use of a common term masks a great diversity of intentions. For example, in Argentina the original intention was to identify those who might be successfully prosecuted; in Chile it was because trials appeared impossible; in South Africa it was to help in the construction of a 'rainbow nation'; and in Guatemala it was to uncover the reality of state atrocities, primarily against indigenous peoples. Initial intentions are one crucial element to consider when examining the mechanisms, but certainly not the only one, for motivations and objectives may change. To take a different example, the form of lustration in Poland may have originated in an aspiration to bring about social reconciliation in the aftermath of communism, but it eventually degenerated so as to become a weapon of extreme intolerance, xenophobia and anti-liberalism. However, this transmutation demonstrates yet another relevant factor to bear in mind: the mechanisms are moulded and reshaped by the environment in which they are implemented and by the interactions between a wide range of forces. This means that they will have some unintended consequences and the results will never be entirely predictable.

What overall conclusions should therefore be drawn from this survey? Firstly, even if we assume that those who devise and implement a particular initiative have positive intentions and objectives (which is not always the case), it would be misguided to believe that the results will necessarily be beneficial or constant across all societies. Secondly, there needs to be a creative and reflective approach, both as to the choice of measures and to the design of each. Thirdly, given the fact that no individual mechanism may have the impact that was intended or a positive outcome, the implementation of a variety of approaches may be wiser than reliance on a single one. Finally, TJ is not a 'one-off' event. Even if a particular mechanism may be regarded as successful in a given society, its impact may soon wear off. Nor is the immediate aftermath of the downfall of a repressive regime or the ending of a civil war always the most appropriate time for all measures. Contending with the past is a long-term necessity.

These concluding remarks have already begun to tackle the crucial question of whether TJ works in practice. As the next two chapters will now show, attempts at evaluation can lead to a minefield of complexity and controversy.

3

Does it Work? Evaluating Transitional Justice

From the beginning of the twenty-first century, TJ has faced challenges from those regarding the claims made by its early advocates as faith-based rather than evidence-based. David Mendeloff made an influential sceptical intervention of this kind in 2004, when he argued that none of the key questions could be answered until further research was done and that studies needed to test the assertions systematically (Mendeloff 2004: 375–6). Others quoted empirical evidence which sought to demonstrate that TJ could even be detrimental to the pursuit of its own goals. In another frequently cited article, based on an analysis of thirty-two civil wars between 1989 and 2003, Jack Snyder and Leslie Vinjamuri argued that trials tended to contribute to the ending of abuses only when those opposed to transition were weak and the domestic infrastructure of justice was already well established. They also maintained that TCs could exacerbate tensions or provide smokescreens for abusive regimes to continue unless the basis for democratic consolidation was already institutionalised. Contradicting the prevailing conventional wisdom of the TJ community, they also claimed that amnesties or other minimal ways of addressing past violations were often the basis for durable peaceful settlements (Snyder and Vinjamuri 2003–4: 19–20, 43–4). Under pressure to justify the field, many advocates of TJ now also accepted that evaluation was necessary. However, this is far from straightforward.

The first question is: *what* should be evaluated? As we have seen, TJ mushroomed after its emergence late in the last century, meaning that it is almost inconceivable to attempt to assess the success of everything implemented in its name. Secondly, what are the *criteria* for determining 'success'? The professed goals of TJ are extremely wide-ranging and include bringing about justice (defined in various ways), seeking accountability, establishing truth, ending impunity, improving human rights and democracy, deterring further atrocities, removing perpetrators, establishing reconciliation and building peace. But these are not always mutually compatible and, above all, are extremely difficult to measure. And, thirdly, *how* should they be evaluated? Should this be through quantitative methods that seek to translate such goals into measurable entities? Or is it preferable to use qualitative or interpretive methods or some kind of critical analysis? And there is normally a relationship between the focus of evaluation (*what* to evaluate) and the approach (*how* to evaluate it). Thus those who attempt to assess the success of TJ as a whole are more likely to turn to quantification, sometimes reinforced through exemplification in case studies, while a smaller scale focus is likely to employ in-depth qualitative or critical approaches. The initial call for evaluation has resulted in a myriad of responses disclosing numerous normative and theoretical questions and answers about the whole field of TJ – what it is and what it should be. And the very term 'evaluation' may narrow the field by implying an exclusively positivist approach to measurement (Ainley 2017: 425).

This chapter starts by considering some general empirical attempts at evaluating TJ and then examines two contrasting mechanisms in greater detail: TCs, which tend to be primarily national, though often with a very significant international input, and the international network of criminal justice. The following chapter then considers two specific perspectives, partially generated by the search for evaluation – those that are 'victim-centred' and those informed by feminist and gendered analysis.

Empirical Evaluations of the Impact of TJ

Some studies seek to determine whether TJ has a significant role in preventing the recurrence of mass atrocities, while others ask more positive questions about its possible impact. Some attempts to 'test' TJ empirically have sought to adopt a wholly detached, dispassionate approach without any explicit normative preferences for the framework of TJ. This was the case, for example, in one influential study, which was stridently quantitative (Lie et al. 2007). It was based on the data of 200 post-conflict cases from 1946 to 2003, and the focus was on 'what worked' rather than on what was morally or legally appropriate. It also took a minimalist definition of peace, which accepted that this might be brought about by repression and deterrence (ibid.: 2–3). The study concluded that, for many variables, the results were weak and rarely statistically significant, but that victory by one side appeared to be the strongest and most consistent variable in the explanation of subsequent peace duration. Trials emerged as the most important type of justice, but the effects of these were very sensitive to the way in which the conflict ended; amnesties tended to reduce the duration of peace, though again the way a conflict ended had an impact on this; and reparations and truth commissions might have a prolonging effect on the duration of peace in a post-conflict society (ibid.: 15–18).

Influential forces were also advocating this kind of 'objective' approach. Governments and other donors who had funded TJ programmes sought value for their money or lessons for the future by seeking concrete information about 'what worked', and the dominant academic tradition of positivism, particularly in the US, held that reputable social science needed to be 'testable' through quantitative evidence. This was given further impetus within TJ by an influential report, supported by the Canadian government, on the effects of TJ mechanisms (Thoms et al. 2008). While this acknowledged an important role for case studies, the main thrust of its recommendations was that empirical claims needed more sustained systematic comparative analysis.

Perhaps in partial response to the quantitative 'turn', various studies by Kathryn Sikkink, first in co-authored work and culminating in her major book *The Justice Cascade* (2011), sought to combine committed engagement in TJ with empirical analysis. While avowing that she was using the data in an objective manner, Sikkink claimed that this nevertheless demonstrated her contention that TJ in general, and trials in particular, were creating a global justice cascade that had put an end to the possibility of impunity for mass atrocities. Despite her powerful advocacy of human rights prosecutions, there is widespread scepticism about the extent to which Sikkink established the validity of her claim. This is partly because of the data itself but also because of her inferences from it. For example, she used prosecutions in quantifying the number and location of trials, attempting to demonstrate that their very existence led to a decline in human rights violations. However, this argument has been criticised since it involved counting incomplete trials, which may have been dropped for political or other reasons or were never intended to bring about verdicts. Perhaps of still greater significance, Sikkink sought to use her conclusions rather tendentiously to refute arguments by realists and sceptics. For example, while many argued that trials could sometimes destabilise or even jeopardise a transition, as for example in Argentina in the 1980s, she claimed that the fact that such trials resumed much later demonstrated that this was not so. However, trials could be threatening in the first period but viable some thirty years later when the new regime had become more stable (McAuliffe 2013b: 117). More generally, Sikkink's conclusions seem too sweeping. She wants to persuade, through a version of constructivist argument, that the human rights movement, harnessed to prosecutions, has brought about fundamental change, both in countries that have staged trials and globally. Despite her protestations to the contrary, this seems to be a monocausal explanation of complex and contradictory phenomena.

Other studies, such as the influential works by Leigh Payne and her co-authors, culminating in *Transitional Justice in Balance* (Olsen et al. 2010a), appear more convincing. Their objective, in a primarily quantitative study, was to explore the relationship between TJ and the subsequent strengthening of human rights and democracy. They used their own database on five forms of TJ (trials, TCs, amnesties, reparations and lustration) for every country in the world from 1970 to 2007 and incorporated all forms of trial, but only those reaching a verdict. Using statistical analyses, including controls for several alternative explanations of the outcomes, they concluded that dealing with past violence led to better outcomes in terms of democracy and human rights than ignoring it, but that none of the mechanisms had this effect in isolation (Olsen et al. 2010b: 993–4). Furthermore, they argued that TCs on their own had a negative effect and that only two combinations were successful: *either* trials and amnesties *or* trials, amnesties and TCs. They thus agreed with Sikkink and Lie, Binningsbø and Gates on the importance of trials but disagreed with them on amnesties, where they came close to the position of Snyder and Vinjamuri.

Describing their conclusions as a 'justice balance', Olsen and her colleagues argued that this suggested a sequenced approach: for example, initial amnesties to provide time for the consolidation of democracy and judicial institutions, followed by trials (2010b: 996–9). Since they suggested that TCs were not essential, this might appear to be a negative finding, but they also had some positive conclusions in this respect, for they argued that commissions could make a positive complementary contribution. For example, those that named perpetrators or required them to confess enhanced the accountability mechanism provided by trials, and democracies that implemented TC recommendations on financial reparations and institutional reforms could contribute to political and economic stability (ibid.: 999–1003).

Payne and her co-authors also made one particularly important contribution. At an earlier stage of TJ, there was a tendency to contrast the various mechanisms in a binary way: was the restorative approach of a TC superior to, or less worthwhile than, the retributive focus of a trial? The 'justice balance' reinforced the argument that a combination of mechanisms was more likely to be effective, that there could be sequencing between them, and that they should be regarded as complementary rather than alternatives. This was also in harmony with the normative arguments for a wide-ranging approach, advocated, for example, by Pablo de Greiff and discussed in chapter 1 (de Greiff 2012). However, important discrepancies remained between the various quantitative studies – for example, whether amnesties tended to have a positive or negative impact. A recent, more general study of the 'anti-atrocity-toolbox', which looked primarily at statistical approaches, was sceptical about whether the data was sufficiently robust to draw clear conclusions (Conley-Zilkic et al. 2016: 25), and different methodologies and data sources have led to different results, with predominantly quantitative approaches failing to resolve several fundamental questions about the impact of TJ. Many doubt whether there is even a theoretical possibility of reaching any certainty about impact (Duggan 2010b).

One obvious reason for this is the relatively short time-frame on which most such studies are inevitably based. This may be highlighted with reference to Germany, which is now often taken as a model for successfully contending with the past. Yet until the 1960s most of the population still regarded the Nuremberg trials solely as rendering victors' justice (Hazan 2006: 27). But there is a more fundamental factor than time alone, for societies are immensely complex phenomena with interactions between numerous forces and actors, embedded in social, cultural, political, historical, economic and international contexts and processes. Repressive regimes or civil wars, and the mass atrocities and large-scale human rights abuses that occur in these circumstances, arise from multiple causes. The idea that an intervention in the sphere of TJ is likely to have an autonomous measurable impact separable from all other factors thus appears unrealistic. This also raises some questions about the data that has typically been used as a test of such impact.

Much of the comparative research has been based on the quest for statistical correlations between TJ and improvements in human rights and democracy or the prevention of new violent conflicts and atrocities. On the surface this might appear quite reasonable, but quantitative data is not entirely 'innocent', and there is an additional problem that the choice of data can already contain an unconscious further bias. In seeking particular correlations, there is an assumption that these are of the greatest possible significance, but this may be questioned. Arguably, evaluation in relation to human rights and democracy and acceptance of the constituent elements within conventional definitions remain embedded in the Western liberal framework that underpinned the original project of TJ. Evaluators in large-scale quantitative approaches tend to rely on covert values even though they may have set out to move beyond such normative approaches (Ainley 2017: 441).

As Dustin Sharp has argued, there are advantages in viewing TJ as one element within the broader goal of bringing about a 'positive peace' – a notion which is equally appropriate for considering both transitional regimes and transitions from civil war (Sharp 2015). Many theorists and practitioners of peacebuilding have long used the concept of positive peace, following Johan Galtung in distinguishing between this and 'negative peace', which refers simply to the absence of war (Galtung 1969, 1990). Galtung also elaborated these notions further by suggesting that positive peace required the eradication of two phenomena that differ from overt physical violence but are underlying preconditions for it: 'structural violence', which inheres in particular social structures, and 'cultural violence', which may legitimise these. These are elusive ideas but may be illustrated as follows. In apartheid South Africa, there was overt physical violence in police brutality against the black majority, but the structural violence existed within the whole system, which was itself maintained through the cultural violence of racial hierarchy.

There are problems in regarding positive peace as an attainable goal, given the fact that all societies contain elements of structural and cultural violence, but it can nevertheless be valuable in exploring the nature and imperfections of particular transitions and pointing out the direction of travel that is necessary. *After Violence: Transitional Justice, Peace and Democracy* (Skaar et al. 2015) is, in my view, an advance on previous studies both because of its method and because it incorporates such ideas. It focuses on four mechanisms – TCs, trials, amnesties and reparations – and four case studies – Angola, Rwanda, Uruguay and Peru. In addition, it establishes a framework for a comparative qualitative approach, focusing particularly on democracy and peace. This both shows sensitivity to context and the differing definitions of peace, democracy and transition and ensures comparability by following the same approach in each case. The four countries were also selected because they varied in the types of transitional mechanisms employed (that is, what the authors were trying to assess the impact *of*); their current degree of peace and democracy (that is, what they were trying to assess the impact *on*) and the major contextual factors at the national, regional and world levels likely to have affected TJ. The qualitative approach was supplemented by some quantitative checks, but the authors were explicit about the limitations of the data.

The study sought to answer the following questions: firstly, whether societies that use TJ mechanisms to hold alleged perpetrators of past crimes accountable become more peaceful, less violent and more democratic than countries that do not; secondly, to what extent peace and democracy are dependent on formal TJ mechanisms; thirdly, how the process by which a TJ mechanism is established and promoted (particularly in terms of national versus international drivers) influences the outcome, and, finally, how, if at all, the various TJ mechanisms differ in their impact (Skaar et al. 2015: 29–59). In relation to the four mechanisms, the authors concluded that reparations, TCs and amnesties had both potentially positive and negative impacts, dependent on the particular circumstances within the countries, but they found no evidence of negative effects for trials. On the basis of these four case studies, their conclusions therefore reinforced the findings of many of the other comparative studies, but with the important proviso that they were not suggesting that trials should necessarily take place at the beginning of a transition. In fact, in the case of Uruguay, their major success story, these were delayed for a considerable period. The other key conclusions included the following points.

Firstly, that the duration and nature of the conflict preceding the transition, the issues at stake and how the conflict ended all shaped the general conditions for future peace and democracy. In particular, Skaar and her colleagues found that the challenges facing governments after internal armed conflict were more complex than those facing post-authoritarian governments, perhaps partly because post-armed conflict governments had less political and institutional capacity to deal adequately with the violations. But they also found that location was important, for the role of the Inter-American Court of Human Rights in Latin America was more significant than any regional body in Africa, and rulings against both Peru and Uruguay played a central role in domestic efforts to eliminate amnesty laws, broadening the scope for criminal prosecutions.

Secondly, context and time were very significant. The periods of authoritarian rule in Uruguay and mixed civil conflict/authoritarian rule in Peru were tied to particular regimes and delimited in time, meaning that TJ could usefully be concentrated on a particular period. Decades of civil war in Angola meant that the periods of violence were far more extensive, and the country opted out of prosecutions and other forms of TJ completely. In Rwanda the balance of power after the genocide was a crucial factor, for the victorious party, the Rwandan Patriotic Front (RPF), was able to address the violations of the genocide as it wished (although in an autocratic way and in a situation which has not led to positive peace).

Thirdly, state-to-citizen violence posed different challenges for post-conflict trust-building than citizen-to-citizen violence, which meant that the situation was now quite different in Uruguay from that in Rwanda, where the genocide had involved ordinary people. Fourthly, as shown by both Uruguay and Peru, previous experience of democracy is an asset for the subsequent reconstruction of democratic institutions and practices, whereas neither Angola nor Rwanda had ever been even quasi-democracies. In the most favourable situations there is also likely to be an interaction effect between institution-building and a willingness and capacity in government to push for and implement TJ. And where courts are well functioning and independent, the possibility of free and fair trials is also higher. Furthermore, in Uruguay this has strengthened judicial capacity, independence, the rule of law and democracy in contrast with countries where weak courts carry out limited or flawed trials, as in Peru, or where there are no trials at all, as in Angola.

Fifthly, civil society can exert pressure for TJ, as in the more democratic societies of Uruguay and Peru, but it played almost no role in relation to TJ in the one-party, autocratic states of Angola and Rwanda. In such cases, if TJ is to occur at all, some other actor must be pushing for it or it will not take place. In Rwanda, both the new regime itself and international actors established it, but in Angola there was no such push either domestically or internationally. Finally, time and sequencing are important in various ways, not only in relation to the length of the conflict or transition period but also in relation to phases in the climate of opinion, both domestically and internationally. In Uruguay, for example, these were conducive to the creation of a change from complete impunity to systematic truth-telling and accountability – although the study condemns the continuation of torture and the vacillation of the Supreme Court in relation to amnesty laws (Skaar 2015: 87, 89). In Angola, in contrast, economic and strategic interests have meant that there has been no international pressure to implement any form of TJ, while there is now a long-term domestic climate of impunity. However, the Angolan civil war ended only in 2002, there are other immense tasks of reconstruction following colonialism and external intervention, and the situation might not be ripe for TJ. Putting the Angolan situation in a comparative context, Skaar, Malca and Eide also note that such mechanisms only began ten years after the transition in Uruguay (2015: 174–94).

After Violence explores very pertinent questions, examining the evidence empirically but with some normative underpinning. It accepts that it is possible to have transitions without TJ and also that this should not be understood simply in terms of formal mechanisms, which may be established for duplicitous reasons. It substantiates a conclusion that, in some circumstances, TJ mechanisms may contribute to the social healing of deeply wounded societies. Depending on the context and processes, they may also make a significant contribution to building democracy and peace in the long run and helping to 'contend with the past'. But I end this section with some additional points.

As noted in chapter 1, almost two decades ago Rama Mani critiqued TJ in both theory and practice for failing to address the specific problems of developing countries, and this remains valid in relation to comparative evaluations. The Global North has played a key role in creating and perpetuating conditions in the Global South that are conducive both to civil wars and to the establishment and continuation of repressive regimes. Furthermore, poorer countries, which are maintained in this situation through the structures and policies of the international economic system, clearly have fewer material resources and skilled personnel to implement either effective TJ systems or the virtuous circle of institutional interactions necessary to underpin meaningful systems of democracy and peace. To maintain that a country's position in the international economy is relevant for any meaningful evaluation of TJ is neither to suggest structural determinism nor to exempt political and economic elites in developing countries from responsibility for repression or atrocities. But simply focusing on national factors under-states some of the key influences, and, as already suggested, providing data solely on democracy and human rights can imply a Western liberal bias.

No data set or index is entirely neutral, but there are other indices which are relevant but have not been widely used in evaluations of TJ. The *Human Development Index* is a composite measure of life expectancy, education and per capita incomes and now also includes an inequality-adjusted measure. All these are relevant when considering different forms of transitions and outcomes. For example, although repressive regimes may sometimes be located in countries at a relatively higher level of development, the majority of recent violent civil wars and episodes of mass atrocities have taken place in developing countries. Significant aspects of successful transition, including in establishing TJ mecha-nisms, may also be accomplished more easily in relatively wealthier states. In respect of the four cases used in *After Violence*, it is therefore notable that, in the report for 2018, Uruguay was categorised as at a very high level of devel-opment and Peru at a high level (respectively at 55th and 89th out of a total of 189 states), while Angola was in the 'medium' and Rwanda in the 'low' category (respectively 147th and 158th) (UNDP 2018). Some of the differences in progress recorded in the study are surely attributable to these differing positions in overall human development.

The Institute for Economics and Peace in Sydney publishes an annual *Global Peace Index*, which also has some relevance. Since 2015 the report has included an overall theory as to how a positive peace incorporates self-sustaining mechanisms and has evaluated states in relation to twenty-four indicators distributed among eight main 'pillars of peace'. Criticisms can certainly be made, both of the indicators themselves and of the way in which the various measures are compiled to bring about an overall figure. Nevertheless, the reports have some telling statistics and conclusions with some striking differences from the rankings in the *Human Development Index*, for many poorer countries are included in the high rankings. This demonstrates that it would be misconceived to suggest any simple correlation between peace and levels of development. Nevertheless, the four cases discussed above are ranked in the same order in the 2018 *Global Peace Index* as in the *Human Development Index*, although none is in the 'low' or 'very low' category: out of a total of 163 states, Uruguay and Peru are in the 'high' category, respectively at 37 and 74, with Angola, and Rwanda in the 'medium' one, respectively at 83 and 103 (Institute for Economics and Peace 2018).

These sets of data reinforce the argument that structural relationships underlie more peaceful societies and that there is complexity and multidimensional causality. Both indices incorporate some elements of human rights and democracy, but only as parts of far larger sets of interactions constituting peace and development. These complex relationships between TJ, development and peace have not normally been highlighted in the comparative studies (see Dancy and Wiebelhaus-Brahm 2015 for a limited step in this direction). In my view, further comparative studies on the impact of TJ, following the example of *After Violence*, would be enriched by greater sensitivity to such factors.

Truth Commissions

Having been 'hyped' as the epitome of TJ, in recent years TCs have been widely criticised and, as already shown, many of the large-scale studies seeking to evaluate TJ have been sceptical about their impact. One major comparative work solely on TCs does not fundamentally counter this stance (Wiebelhaus-Brahm 2010). This combines a qualitative approach to four cases with a large-scale quantitative study, and the conclusion is hardly a ringing endorsement of the beneficial effects of such commissions. While the case studies

– South Africa, Chile, El Salvador and Uganda – appeared to show that some advances in relation to institutional aspects of democracy and human rights protection could probably be attributed to the TCs, the work also argues that they were then frequently undermined by crime and continuing violence (ibid.: 18, 153). The results of the quantitative study were still more negative, suggesting that human rights violations tended to increase in the aftermath of TCs, which had no statistically significant effect on democracy (ibid.: 21). Certainly it seems reasonable to suggest that TCs are neither necessary nor sufficient for the inculcation of a human rights culture and that they tend to mark the end of efforts to deal with the past rather than the beginning (Brahm 2007: 26–8). But if it is unreliable to derive firm conclusions about the impact of TJ in general by focusing on measurable outcomes, this applies still more to individual mechanisms such as TCs.

Another analysis of TCs as a whole, by Onur Bakiner, makes more use of qualitative insights. While rebutting excessive claims about the benefits of TCs and offering a cautious rather than a celebratory evaluation, Bakiner seeks to dispel some undue scepticism. He stresses the importance of the initial factors, arguing that the inclusivity of the commission's creation process, and particularly the extent to which civil society actors are involved in its establishment, is a key determinant of its subsequent impact (Bakiner 2014: 14; 2016: 49). Similarly, the nature of the specific mandate is of great importance, for this simultaneously enables the commission and constrains it, and both the mandate and the composition determine the extent and manner in which the TC can discover facts about the past and construct a narrative about it. The process is also dynamic, with commissioners and their staff normally having considerable agency in how they interpret their mandate, carry out their tasks, decide what to include in the final report, and interact with different sectors of the society. This can lead to surprising twists, both because mandates are sometime vague and because commissioners make a difference as a result of their own backgrounds, interests, experiences, world-views and skills (Bakiner 2016: 61). And, whatever the original nature of the mandate, wider dissatisfaction about this can provoke changes in the longer term. For example, the fact that investigations into torture and exile were excluded from the terms of the initial TC in Chile in 1990 motivated activist mobilisation, which helped to ensure that these issues were addressed in subsequent official and unofficial TCs (ibid.: 50).

One criticism that has been made of TCs is that they tend to appropriate a particular version of the past for nation-building purposes, providing a liberal interpretation that seeks to replace or suppress more radical alternative perspectives (Grandin 2005; Grandin and Klubock 2007). Bakiner holds that the reality is more complex, accepting, for example, that this critique is apt in relation to Chile and Argentina, but that this is not always the case. Citing Guatemala and Peru, he suggests that the 'truth' of TCs often delegitimises governmental policies.

The two situations differed. The Guatemalan TC (the Commission for Historical Clarification, 1997–9) was created as a response to the massive violations and atrocities committed during the thirty-six-year internal conflict, from 1960 until the UN's brokered peace agreement of 1996. From the mid-1950s until the 1970s there had been increasing state repression in response to unrest, but in 1982 the Guatemalan military, backed by all governmental and judicial institutions, had turned to far more extreme measures, and the TC reported that over 200,000 people had subsequently been killed – overwhelmingly by the state. In contrast, the Peruvian Commission for Truth and Reconciliation (2001–3), reporting on the extreme violence in the last twenty years of the previous century, revealed that state and non-state actors shared responsibility for the atrocities. In 1980 the Shining Path, a group inspired by Maoism, had launched an armed uprising against the military dictatorship, using brutal and terroristic methods, but the state response was also ruthless. By 2000 there had been up to 77,552 deaths, with hundreds of thousands of displaced persons. The Shining Path was responsible for 54 per cent of the deaths, another revolutionary movement for 1.5 per cent of them, and pro-state forces for the rest.

The similarity between the Guatemalan and Peruvian situations was that of extreme structural inequality and racism against the indigenous peoples, and the TCs highlighted this. The Guatemalan commission thus noted that 83 per cent of victims of the state violence were indigenous and that, in the four regions most affected by the violence, acts of genocide against the Mayan people had been committed. Similarly, the Peruvian TC commission stressed the fact that 40 per cent of the deaths and disappearances were in the remote Ayacucho region in the Andes inhabited by indigenous peoples. Bakiner thus suggests that, by emphasising the relationship between these systemic inequalities and violence, the TCs did not produce a convenient truth.

Some aspects of this interpretation might be questioned. For example, as discussed later, there are unusual features in the Guatemalan TC which explain its critical approach and willingness to speak out. It may also be argued that the Peruvian TC was quite guarded in some respects. Its task was complicated by the fact that, following the virtual defeat of the revolution, the dictator, President Alberto Fujimori, had already set up so-called TJ measures in his final period in office between 1992 and 2000, although he was deeply implicated in state violence. The new commission was quite different but did not totally challenge the prevailing narrative, in which the victims were represented as ordinary Peruvians, the state as their protector, and terrorist groups as the sole perpetrators. It thus refused to acknowledge that former members of the Shining Path group and their relatives could also be victims. Yet it simultaneously countered this through the statistics it published and by referring to structural factors as explanations of the violence (Malca 2015: 103–10). Overall, the two examples therefore uphold the key point that TCs cannot simply be regarded as mouthpieces for governments which promulgate sanitised versions of history.

Another frequent criticism of TCs has been that they are a covert means of securing amnesties, thereby also avoiding judicial processes. Here, again, Bakiner makes an important contribution in setting the record straight. In fact, only in two cases, that of South Africa and Liberia, did the TCs grant or recommend amnesties, and the South African Truth and Reconciliation Commission dismissed or rejected about 88 per cent of the amnesty applications; many perpetrators did not testify at all. The design of TCs curtails their judicial powers, but the failure to prosecute on any large scale stems less from the commissions or amnesty laws accompanying them than from the unwillingness of the judiciary or political leaders to proceed. It is true that many politicians, military and security forces, and armed groups have sometimes favoured TCs in the hope that they would replace, or distract attention from, prosecutions, but not that the commissions have generally either advocated impunity or undermined demands for trials (Bakiner 2014: 25–30).

Bakiner provides a judicious defence of TCs, but it is still debatable whether any generic evaluation is possible. He concludes that the key factor in whether they bring about any long-term progress towards democracy and human rights is the existence of sustained and continuing pressure by civil society organisations (Bakiner 2014: 30). This is an important finding, and the extent of civil society mobilisation may be a significant variable for otherwise similar societies. But it is surely questionable whether the possibilities for civil society mobilisation and impact exist everywhere, as shown in *After Violence* in relation to the discussion of Rwanda and Angola. In differing ways, both Kenya and Nepal highlight limitations in emphasising the impact of civil society in isolation from other factors.

Following Kenya's independence in 1963 from colonial rule by Britain, which had been responsible for extreme atrocities in the 1950s, both President Jomo Kenyatta and his successor, Daniel arap Moi, instituted repressive dictatorships. There were mass human rights violations reinforced by 'divide-and-rule' policies among the diverse communities in the country. A corrupt ruling elite also controlled the economy, bringing together the public and private sectors (Branch 2011: 122–3). However, this system faced increasing challenges during the 1990s with the development of an active and significant NGO movement, which played a central role in moves towards the promotion of human rights and democratisation and finally ended Moi's dictatorship in 2002 (Hansen and Sriram 2015: 420). Civil society organisations also called for accountability for past abuses and the end of impunity, supporting the initiative of the new president, Mwai Kibaki, in setting up a task force in 2003 on the establishment of a TC. This conducted broad consultations and recommended that it should cover the whole period since independence in 1963 to investigate 'systemic patterns or state policies ... to abrogate the rights of Kenyans' (quoted in Naughton 2016a: 59). However, Kibaki ignored the recommendation (Lanegran 2015: 50–1).

The circumstances that preceded the eventual establishment of a TC (the Truth, Justice and Reconciliation Commission) five years later differed considerably, for they followed the outbreak of extreme violence in the aftermath of the elections held at the end of 2007. These had reignited long-term conflicts over land, power and wealth, focusing on ethnicity, with Kibaki, the incumbent president, seeking to rig the election results and also inciting Gikuyu violence against other communities. In the ensuing crisis, at least 1,333 people were killed, thousands of women were raped, property was destroyed, and more than 500,000 people were forced to flee from their homes (Branch 2011: 271–5). All this precipitated external mediation led by the former UN Secretary-General Kofi Annan, who brought the major party leaders together in a National Dialogue (the TC followed from this). At this stage there was still a very substantial civil society sector exerting considerable pressure, resulting in an exceptionally wide mandate that included 'major economic crimes, in particular grand corruption, historical land injustices or irregular acquisition of land' (quoted in Naughton 2016a: 61).

The commission was beset with intractable difficulties from the start, not least of which was the fact that its chair, appointed by the president, was himself accused of human rights violations and possible crimes. This led to a long deadlock within the commission until April 2012, and by then it had lost legitimacy and support in civil society; some NGOs were even working against it and holding it in contempt (Naughton 2016a: 64; Hansen and Sriram 2015: 420). Yet the most crippling obstruction was that of the government and political elite in general. As the commission itself noted in its reflective final report, there was no real co-operation because of a reassertion of vested interests, a backsliding from reform, corruption, accumulation of wealth, a desire for continued power and a lack of political will, and 'the absence of a clean break with the past' (Naughton 2016a: 65). Manipulation by the political leadership undermined any potential for the TC to bring about significant change in Kenyan society.

The major problem was that civil society organisations were operating in an environment in which political elites had evaded significant control since independence and successfully undermined the ideas of the NGO sector in order to put it on the defensive. This does not mean that the commission was unimportant, for it remains a valuable resource for the future if major reforms lead to a situation in which a Kenyan government genuinely wishes to contend with the past. But this example shows that a strong civil society movement cannot ensure the effectiveness of a TC when governments and elites remain sufficiently powerful and determined to prevent this.

In a quite different way, the TC in Nepal also demonstrates the limitations of civil society in a hostile environment. In this extremely poor, overwhelmingly rural and mountainous country, the ten-year civil war between Maoist and governmental forces from 1996 to 2006 led to more than 13,000 deaths, mainly of civilians, and also torture, extrajudicial killings and approximately 1,300 forced disappearances. There were violations on both sides, but the security services used enforced disappearances as a counter-insurgency measure, and the majority of victims were accused of sympathising with the Maoists (Naughton 2016b: 74). This led to a very active movement by victims' families, who staged hunger strikes, lodged reports with the police and sought action in the courts from an early stage in the conflict. Their demands for information about what had happened, and for some form of redress, became a rallying point for all those supporting accountability, and their pressure intensified at the end of the war (Farasat and Hayner 2009: 20). Once again, the results of the subsequent TC (the Truth and Reconciliation Commission) were very dispiriting, but not because of a lack of civil society mobilisation.

The proposal for such a commission appeared suddenly as an expedient for the major political parties to maintain impunity and protect themselves against prosecution. Without consultation with the wider civil society movements, both governmental forces and the Maoists now saw this as a way of securing an amnesty for past atrocities. There was no organic Nepalese demand for a TC, but these had become a default mechanism for international human rights and TJ activists, and this facilitated some cynical manoeuvres and procrastination by political leaders. Only in February 2015 did the government finally form both a Commission of Investigation on Enforced Disappeared Persons and the TC, which began their work more than a year later. Many victim and civil society organisations remained alienated from both commissions (International Commission of Jurists 2017). There was still civil society mobilisation, but the mechanisms that were set up were not the product of an indigenous social or political movement and were widely, and justifiably, regarded as a ploy to evade accountability.

The cases of Kenya and Nepal suggest that civil society mobilisation is only one factor in influencing the impact of a TC, which cannot be isolated from the overall constellation of forces, institutions and structures, both domestic and international. Since there are multiple interactions, the results in any situation are only partially predictable, and 'lessons' from one case are not easily transferable to another, even when many aspects of the context may appear similar. The fact that the influence of international TJ may have been largely negative in the poor and mountainous society of Nepal does not therefore mean that this is always the case. This may be illustrated by turning once again to the Guatemalan TC, for here the international role was positive.

The UN Secretary-General appointed the chair of the commission, a German law professor, who in turn nominated the two other members, one of whom had to be a Guatemalan 'of irreproachable conduct' and the other an academic. Ninety per cent of the funding was provided from international sources, the research, analysis and support staff comprised 127 internationals (alongside 142 Guatemalans), many of whom were drawn from UN missions, and the logistics and finances were also arranged by the UN Office for Project Services (Rothenberg 2016: xxxvi). The commission was not representative of Guatemalan society or rooted in civil society movements, and its mandate was very narrow – to clarify the human rights violations and to foster tolerance and preserve the memory of the victims.

Yet the commissioners succeeded in overcoming much of the deep initial mistrust of victims' groups and gathered more than 7,300 testimonies, including those from some of the most isolated and remote communities. This may have been facilitated by the fact that the commissioners made it clear that their objective was not to whitewash the regime. This was confirmed in their final report, which argued that the regime had always been 'racist in its precepts and practices' and that the violence was fundamentally directed by the state 'against the excluded, the poor and above all, the Mayan people', as well as against those who fought for justice and social equality (CEH 1999: 17). Of course, this does not mean that it overcame the climate of impunity in Guatemala, and important restrictions were imposed on it, but it does suggest that an independent and externally led TC can sometimes transcend the circumstances of its creation (Reátegui 2016: 25–31).

If Nepal illustrates the weakness of international sponsorship of a TC and the Guatemalan example suggests its strengths, the Sierra Leonean case reveals yet another variation: international actors both encouraging and partially undermining a commission.

The Sierra Leonean civil war began in 1991 with an armed insurgency by the Revolutionary United Front (RUF), under Foday Sankoh, and formally ended in 2002 after his defeat. Although the country was desperately poor, it possessed extremely valuable mineral resources, particularly diamonds, and control of these was a major factor in the war, which killed approximately 70,000 people and displaced 2.6 million out of a total population of just over 6 million. Among repellent atrocities were the forced recruitment of child soldiers, mass rape, sexual slavery and amputations (Ainley et al. 2015).

The TC (Truth and Reconciliation Commission, 2002–4) was established as a result of the 1999 Lomé Peace Agreement, which was negotiated between the government and the RUF and made Sankoh vice-president. Lomé was accompanied by an amnesty and promoted reconciliation through the TC. This had many innovative features, including separate proceedings for young people and extensive work on sexual and gender-based violence. But it was conceived at a time of stalemate in the war, and the military balance subsequently shifted rapidly, particularly with a British intervention in 2000. With the defeat of Sankoh, the Sierra Leonean government and its principal backers, the US and the UK, established a quite different instrument of TJ – the Special Court for Sierra Leone. This focused on prosecutions of those associated with Sankoh, among them his principal backer, Charles Taylor, the president of Liberia. The court became the international and governmental priority, with extensive funding, while the TC was starved of resources. The establishment of the Special Court also terminated the amnesty, a principal tenet of the TC, thus rendering its task particularly difficult by deterring people from testifying in fear that they might subsequently face prosecution.

Nevertheless, the TC remained a significant instrument for TJ in the country.

In an important comparative study of the Peruvian and Sierra Leonean commissions, Rebekka Friedman (2017) highlights the difficulties in any straightforward evaluation of TCs and stresses both the significance and complexity of the interactions between formal mechanisms and local contexts. In Sierra Leone there was a strong pre-existing emphasis on the idea of reconciliation, the primary value promoted by the TC. But harmony with existing attitudes did not mean that it had a significant impact because of its inadequacies in terms of its formal discourse, slow procedures, insufficient outreach, lack of concrete action and obscure relationship with the Special Court. People turned instead to a locally based alternative project in the Fambul Tok (family talk) circles, which were embedded in traditional cultural forms, and also promoted reconciliation in various practical ways, including through community farms.

The situation was quite different in Peru, where the dominant attitudes among the indigenous populations were of alienation and a demand for redress. Here the commission perhaps generated still more anger than already existed by identifying the state's long-term marginalisation of the most mountainous region and those of indigenous descent as a key underlying cause of the conflict. Acting as a catalyst for alternative memories and raising public awareness of the long-term structural injustices, the commission itself increasingly focused on victims and demands for redress. Paradoxically, therefore, the Peruvian commission probably had a greater impact than that in Sierra Leone because it generated debate and demands for criminal justice, which inevitably also drew in the protagonists, including the military. On the other hand, the shortcomings of the TC in Sierra Leone led to the counter-movement of the Fambul Tok, which also stimulated a critical interest in reconciliation and peacebuilding at local level. Such subtle chains of reaction and counter-reaction operate elsewhere as well, suggesting difficulties in any simple evaluations of particular TCs as successes or failures.

Friedman's study also raises wider questions about assumptions that often underlie judgements about the goals of TCs. Whereas the notion of 'reconciliation' tends to be taken as a linear process in which greater trust and agreement develop over time, she argues that it can be an open-ended process, which does not necessitate any shared views of the past or direct contact between the antagonists and may even cause further division and conflict. It simply requires a limited form of belief by the parties that they have more to gain by pursuing grievances through a shared process than outside it. Conflict should not therefore be taken as the antithesis of reconciliation, but it may be an integral part of it (Friedman 2017: 177–8). But nor should it be taken as an overriding goal in itself, for procedural reconciliation of this kind, which serves as a barometer for conflict, may also mask and legitimise continuing injustice, and it therefore needs to be accompanied by more fundamental forms of transformation (ibid.: 186). Wider issues about the evaluation of TCs – their relationship with the socioeconomic aspects of TJ – also arise from the study.

As discussed in the previous chapter, problems associated with material reparations are generally a major cause of dissatisfaction or disillusionment among victims, and in both Peru and Sierra Leone such feelings had a negative effect on their attitudes to the TCs. Friedman observes that it may be a mistake to link reparations with TCs. Once participation in a mechanism intended to promote dialogue and truth is apparently 'incentivised' with an expectation of reparations, it can, she suggests, detract from the process and its perceived value. In both countries, individuals from marginalised communities testified before reparations were on the agenda but then re-evaluated their engagement in the light of later discussions about material benefits and their own continuing marginalisation. In Sierra Leone, further problems arose when victims came to believe that ex-combatants were testifying in the expectation of such gains (Friedman 2017: 185). This raises one further general issue: whether TCs should be expected to address structural and historical forms of injustice.

Friedman fears that incorporating these issues into TCs can overburden them, shifting the nature of their work and perhaps diverting attention from global responsibility and accountability for the situation (2017: 182, 184). Furthermore, they have limited resources, capacity and time to deal with the tasks assigned to them, and structural violence is normally deeply embedded in societies, meaning that radical recommendations for its alleviation may threaten the interests of dominant elites, further undermining the prospects for a stable transition. The particular problems confronted by the Peruvian TC in relation to reparations were discussed in the previous chapter, as were some of the controversies about the relationships between reparations and development. Friedman's point about elite resistance to TCs attempting to tackle structural injustice is also pertinent, and the findings of the commission in Kenya, which implicated past leaders in economic crimes, were one of the numerous catalysts for its subversion (cited in Naughton 2016a: 66).

Yet many TCs, including the South African Truth and Reconciliation Commission, have been justifiably criticised for failing to address structural injustices adequately. Avoidance of key questions about socioeconomic inequalities will raise concerns about the adequacy of the TC, both in the consciousness of those most adversely affected by the status quo and as a means of promoting a more positive future. There are also difficulties with the idea of a division of labour under which the government should address general issues of development and social justice, while the commission concentrates on overt violence and abuses. For governments will normally avoid tackling the structural issues, and popular opinion will also tend to blame the commissions for such failures. TCs thus reflect a major tension within TJ as a whole.

What, then, is the overall conclusion of this section? A recent study of TCs argued that they are shaped more by the wider social and political context in which they are established than they themselves shape that context (Rowen 2017: 163). In many respects, this viewpoint is endorsed here, for the complex interactions between commissions and the multiple forces that affect their work have been emphasised. Yet, as demonstrated, TCs may nevertheless have significance in many ways, and lessons about contending with the past may be learned from them. Overall, both extreme optimism and undue scepticism are equally misplaced, and it is misguided to generalise too much about their impact.

International and 'Internationalised' Criminal Justice

Trials and prosecutions have already been discussed, but this section focuses particularly on international and 'internationalised' forms of criminal justice. These include the international criminal tribunals for Rwanda and the former Yugoslavia, the various hybrid courts, and the ICC itself. Each of these is different, including in the extent to which the main objective is to develop international law or to focus on the domestic situation within particular countries; and each of them has been influenced by specific objectives. Any form of evaluation is therefore particularly complex.

Some claims by advocates of international justice are unconvincing. For example, the notion that the ICC has a serious deterrent effect on would-be perpetrators of war crimes, crimes against humanity and genocide seems very unlikely. Between its establishment in 2002 and 2018 there had been forty-two defendants, but only eight convictions. Mass atrocities result from a variety of causes, while deterrence depends on a strong degree of certainty that a particular form of behaviour will lead to a definite sanction (Cronin-Furman 2013). Given this low number of convictions in comparison with the total number of egregious violations, the ICC does not meet the conditions for deterrence. On the other hand, some criticisms made by detractors of international criminal justice are certainly too narrow. For example, the costs of the International Criminal Tribunal for Rwanda were extremely high – estimated at $2 billion for only ninety-three indictments and sixty-one prison sentences. It is legitimate to ask whether this amount of money could have been spent more productively in other ways, but it is inadequate simply to take a cost-accounting approach. This would ignore the fact that the tribunal convicted twenty-six people of at least one count of genocide, crimes against humanity or war crimes and also developed international criminal law. Establishing law and norms in relation to the worst mass atrocity crimes were key objectives, and this must form part of any assessment of the tribunal. Yet political as well as judicial motivations and objectives have also been important, and sometimes dominant, in all forms of international and internationalised justice. Any idea that these reflect a pure form of universal justice has never been realised, and is not realisable. This section therefore considers them from a perspective that regards their political role as inescapable.

All forms of internationalised and international courts have been widely criticised for subordinating local interests to those of the major powers, which have often displayed blatant forms of hypocrisy. One early example of this was when the US simultaneously threatened Croatia and Serbia with economic reprisals if they refused to co-operate with the International Criminal Tribunal for the former Yugoslavia, but also if they ratified the ICC statute, which the administration of George W. Bush opposed (Hazan 2006: 34). Similarly, more pressure was placed on Yugoslavia (above all, Serbia) than Rwanda in the two tribunals, partly because the US regarded Serbia as the aggressor and favoured the new regime in Rwanda. Serbian nationalists have therefore always claimed that the tribunal was one-sided, and surveys conducted throughout the 2000s have suggested that an overwhelming majority of Serbs, both in Serbia itself and in the Serbian Republic in Bosnia and Herzegovina, believed it to be biased and untrustworthy. A detailed study partially refutes and partially upholds such claims: it maintains that the trials themselves were conducted in a legally proper way but argues that the tribunal was nevertheless flawed, both because of the political considerations behind its establishment and as regards the question of whom to charge (Ford 2013: 46–51, 105–9).

The International Criminal Tribunal for Rwanda arguably weighed the scales in favour of the post-1994 government even in the founding statute, which stipulated that its purpose was to address the genocide rather than atrocity crimes in general. Subsequent attempts to urge the prosecutor to investigate the crimes of the Tutsi-led rebel army were rebuffed, but this has led to a widely held perception that the tribunal has reinforced the aim of the current Tutsi-led government to attribute exclusive guilt to the Hutus (Schabas 2012: 64, 79; Longman 2017: 282, 309, 333). Other forms of manipulation by the major powers have occurred with hybrid courts, as in the case of Sierra Leone, where the whole agenda for the court seems to have followed a deal between the UK and the US, with the mandates determined politically, partially to bring about regime change in neighbouring Liberia. Consequently, consideration of anything except the actions of a small number of individuals already determined to be 'evil' was ruled out (Mahony 2015: 77–100; Nesiah 2016: 42). Such partisan behaviour has clearly been detrimental to the whole reputation of 'internationalised' criminal justice.

Yet even critics have agreed that there have also been positive results. In particular, it is widely accepted that court cases have led to far greater documentation about, and acknowledgement of, the atrocities than would otherwise have been the case. Despite the fact that the Rwandan government used the International Criminal Tribunal for its own ends, this played a key role in establishing that there had been a genocide (Hazan 2006: 30). Similarly, Jelena Subotić, who has made very forceful and effective criticisms of the International Criminal Tribunal for the former Yugoslavia, suggests that it had three significant effects. Firstly, the tribunal 'sucked out' some of the worst perpetrators and contributed to political stability, and, without its existence, Slobodan Milošević might have been able to re-establish his power in Serbia in 2000. Secondly, the international trials provide a resource for the future, when there may be a greater domestic political will to tackle the issue of past violence. Thirdly, a society needs to become convinced that human rights abuses, war crimes and genocide are wrong, and the tribunal contributed to bringing this about (Subotić 2009: 191). As already noted in chapter 2, the two tribunals contributed to the development of international criminal law in relation to rape and sexual violence. Hybrid courts also had some positive effects in this respect, with the Special Court for Sierra Leone breaking down previous barriers to prosecution in such areas as sexual slavery and the recruitment of child soldiers (Oosterveld 2015: 134–42). However, opinion is deeply divided about other aspects of this court, both because it failed to engage the population as a whole (Ainley et al. 2015: 267–8) and because it prosecuted only rebel groups and civil defence forces, but not government or army personnel (Arnould and Sriram 2014: 5).

This leads to a further, more general, problem in the whole sphere of international and internationalised criminal justice: cynical and opportunistic behaviour by the states themselves, with domestic political elites sometimes hijacking or perverting the courts. One particularly notorious case is that of Hun Sen, the autocratic leader of the Cambodian regime, who succeeded in blocking the work of the Extraordinary Chambers in the Courts of Cambodia in relation to the genocide of 1975–9 and using the legal process to his own advantage (McCargo 2011). Domestic nationalists have also manipulated international criminal justice in relation to the former Yugoslavia.

Milošević's own demagogic tirades and the general way in which Serbian nationalists mobilised support by constantly claiming that the international criminal tribunal was part of a wider Western conspiracy against the country are well known. But forces in both Croatia and Bosnia and Herzegovina also used it for their own purposes. In the Croatian case, for example, the international criminal tribunal's prosecution claimed that the military action in 1995 ('Operation Storm') had been a 'joint state criminal enterprise aimed at removing the entire Serb population from Croatia' (quoted in Subotić 2009: 100). But it focused particularly upon the demand that General Ante Gotovina, who had played a leading role in the operation, should be handed over to the court for war crimes and crimes against humanity. Croatia's eventual co-operation on this case cleared the last obstacle for its major international policy goal – eventual membership of the EU.[1] However, the Croatian political elites continued to reject the charge that Operation Storm had been a criminal action; they claimed it was a foundational heroic battle, thereby perpetuating a nationalist mythology and advancing the interests of the state (ibid.: 99–101). In different ways, nationalist forces in all three countries used the international criminal tribunal (and, in the case of Bosnia and Herzegovina, the successor body, the special War Crimes Chamber) to avoid contending with the past.

In late 2017, two dramatic events demonstrated the continuation of this phenomenon. When, on 22 November, Ratko Mladić, chief of staff of the army of the Serb Republic in Bosnia and Herzegovina, was finally convicted of genocide, war crimes and crimes against humanity, the Serbian leader in the country declared that the whole purpose of the International Criminal Tribunal was to demonise Serbs, on whom he called to 'forever erase every mention of the court's proceedings from their school textbooks' (Borger 2017). Similarly, a week later, after Slobodan Praljak, a Croatian former general, poisoned himself in the courtroom following his sentencing for war crimes for a joint criminal enterprise to ethnically cleanse Bosnian Muslims, Croatian nationalists mobilised to support his reputation. The Catholic archbishop and prime minister both denounced the injustice of the court's verdict, parliament held a minute's silence in

---

[1] In April 2011 Gotovina and one co-defendant were found guilty, while another was acquitted. Following a successful appeal, the two guilty verdicts were overturned.

honour of the deceased war criminal, and, on the day of an official commemoration, citizens were given free transport to the event (Drakulić 2017). Of course, not all members of any of these communities share nationalist views, but clearly the legal processes did not bring about reconciliation. However, it would be naïve to expect an international or internationalised court to be sufficient to achieve any dramatic results in a situation in which domestic elites are mobilising against it.

Unlike many of the hybrid courts, both the International Criminal Tribunals were set up in situations of ongoing conflict, and this is very often also the case in situations in which the ICC has carried out investigations and indictments. But there is considerable debate as to whether international criminal justice can make any major contribution without the prior establishment of some form of peace or at least stability. Many have been dubious about this (Engstrom 2013: 41–61), and negative judgements about the effectiveness of international legal intervention in such situations have been reinforced by the failure of attempts to take such action in Syria. The ICC is therefore in a particularly difficult situation: negative interventions can harm its reputation overall, and several such failures have had a cumulative effect. Such judgements may also sometimes be made for reasons that have little to do with the quality of the intervention. Thus, to take an obvious current issue, the ICC's reputation in many parts of Africa is poor, not necessarily because of clear 'failures' but because it is held to be anti-African, or imperialist, or subservient to a hypocritical Security Council.

Opinion on the ICC has tended to be rather polarised, precisely because of the boundary problems between justice and politics. On one side, there have been those who promote a view of the court as a generally disinterested actor (Mendes 2010), while, in contrast, some stress its role as a puppet of the major Western powers, and particularly the US (Mamdani 2009; Glasius 2009). Neither of these perspectives provides an entirely adequate depiction of the reality, as demonstrated by David Bosco in a rich historical and interpretive analysis of the ICC. This examines the relationships of dependency and control that constrain and sometimes undermine the ICC, highlighting its attempts to transcend these limitations, but concluding that double standards are embedded in existing global structures, with the Court more likely to reflect these than to transcend them (Bosco 2014: 177–89). This is evident in its tortuous relationship with the major states, its relative lack of resources, and its need to secure the co-operation of the states in which it intervenes for information, enforcement and arrests. Any intervention in ongoing violence will necessarily be a factor in the dynamics of the conflict itself, but to ask in advance about the possible impact of the ICC is to pose a political question. However, its first chief prosecutor, Luis Moreno Ocampo, constantly insisted that political considerations could not affect its decisions (Moreno Ocampo 2008: 1, quoted in Wegner 2015: 305). This was an avowal that the ICC was focused on a single-minded pursuit of 'justice', irrespective of whether or not this impeded or advanced the cause of peace in any specific situation, and was clearly oversimplified.

The ICC's first two judicial interventions were both the result of referrals by the leaders of the countries in question – by Uganda in December 2003 and by the Democratic Republic of Congo (DRC) in March 2004. The case of Uganda will be discussed further below, but some points about the DRC may be highlighted. The country was embroiled in large-scale domestic and regional violent conflict. This was initially triggered in 1996 by some of the consequences of the genocide in Rwanda, but the fighting was largely about the control of the country's massive mineral resources and resulted in approximately 3.9 million deaths between 1998 and 2004. The ICC intervention was never entirely principled. Firstly, it avoided the danger of alienating the president of the DRC, Joseph Kabila, or the major powers, which were currently supporting him, by focusing on a region far removed from the area in which government involvement in atrocities might have been revealed. Secondly, it prosecuted Thomas Lubanga (the first person sentenced by the Court) for three counts of war crimes in relation to the enlistment and forced participation of children in fighting. Still more serious crimes had been perpetrated, but a successful prosecution on this charge appeared more likely. A conviction on the lesser charge was designed to help build support for the Court, but the nature of the ICC intervention may have undermined its credibility with some of the most affected local populations because of the failure to bring about accountability for those primarily responsible for the mass atrocities (Clark 2008: 39–42). The Lubanga trial was flawed for many reasons, although the ICC responded positively and learned several lessons from its shortcomings in this case (Freedman 2017).

Any genuine attempt to evaluate the ICC must surely recognise that it is operating within a highly constraining international environment and that it is unlikely ever to be the key determinant of the eventual outcome in any particular conflict. Two recent illuminating studies, with overlapping aims, methods and conclusions, are particularly helpful since they seek to assess the contribution that ICC judicial interventions have made to peace and peacebuilding (Wegner 2015; Kersten 2016). Both adopt a broadly political perspective and use case studies (each examines Uganda, while Wegner also deals with Sudan and Kersten with Libya) to elucidate more general conclusions. Both clearly regard the ICC as important, but neither eulogises it. Both demonstrate its tendency to deal with complex conflicts through a simplistic narrative of 'good versus evil' and argue that it needs to strengthen its capacity to analyse its own impact and its potential to contribute to peace (Kersten 2016: 197–8; Wegner 2015: 12, 329–32). Both constantly stress its role as a political actor, and Wegner also insists that it needs to acknowledge the contradictions between political and legal aspects rather than continuing with the pretence that it is simply judicial. His argument that there is space for greater flexibility without damaging the integrity of law (ibid.: 306, 329–30) is surely important, and some of the analysis in each work demonstrates the dangers of an overly rigid approach. Although they differ on one crucial episode in relation to Uganda, the two authors share most aspects of their assessment.[2]

Since 2002, the Ugandan government had been engaged in a particularly intensive military campaign to bring about the final defeat of the Lord's Resistance Army (LRA), which had first begun its rebellion in 1987. This brutal movement, under Joseph Kony, which practised terror and was notorious for abducting children to fight, had initially arisen in the north of Uganda, where there were many legitimate grievances against state policies. Both Kersten and Wegner agree that the Ugandan president, Yoweri Museveni, used the ICC largely to uphold a one-sided approach by focusing exclusively on crimes committed by the LRA and maintaining impunity for his own forces, which had also committed numerous atrocities. Both also argue that Museveni's marginalisation of Northern Uganda and confrontational approach had played a major role in creating the context for a rebellion. More generally, their central point is that the ICC will have only a limited impact in addressing atrocities given the interaction of so many other factors, but that it also needs to be more cognisant of the potential effects of its interventions on the domestic situations of the countries in question.

One final factor to be considered is the wider political impact of the ICC. In his analysis of its role in Sudan, Wegner confirms the widespread belief that the attempt to prosecute the president of Sudan on multiple charges, including that of genocide, was crucial in reinforcing African perceptions of the ICC as a neo-colonial court (2015: 297). While charges

---

[2] This concerned the Juba peace negotiations between the government and the Lord's Resistance Army from 2006 until 2008. Contradicting many accounts, but based on his own field research and overall analysis, Kersten regards the role of the ICC in relation to the Juba talks as broadly positive (2016: 82–113), while Wegner argues that it was negative and perhaps played a decisive role in their eventual failure (2015: 233–68).

of imperialism have been made, the main argument, which is wholly justified, has been that the Security Council is guilty of double standards in focusing on Africa while the most powerful permanent member states have not signed or not ratified the Rome Statute. The crisis escalated during 2016, with Burundi, The Gambia and South Africa all notifying the Court of their intentions of withdrawing from it. In fact, only Burundi had done so by 2018; The Gambia formally reversed its decision in February 2017 and South Africa's position remains uncertain. But the tensions with the ICC transcend individual states, for in January 2017 the African Union passed a motion endorsing an 'ICC Withdrawal Strategy'. In fact, many AU members do not want withdrawal and may have supported the document primarily as a negotiating strategy. A compromise may therefore be possible (Kersten 2017). But what impact might any such eventuality have on international and internationalised criminal justice?

Any substantial withdrawal from its jurisdiction by African states would certainly be a major setback to the aspirations behind the establishment of the ICC. In fact, if this is taken as the embodiment of international criminal justice, it might appear to be a blow for TJ more generally. Yet there are also good reasons for regarding African withdrawals in a less dramatic way. As suggested earlier, the two International Criminal Tribunals, the hybrid courts and the ICC may all be regarded as elements within a more general system, and there are also other components. In particular, as already noted, the Inter-American Human Rights system has become a major actor in promoting TJ in Latin America (Engstrom 2016; forthcoming). This suggests a similar possibility for the African Union, in which regional systems might work in a complementary rather than an antagonistic relationship with the ICC. This could appeal to many African leaders, who accept the norms theoretically informing the work of the Court but have objections to elements in its approach. After a period in which the system of hybrid courts seemed to have been abandoned, there has also been a recent resurgence,[3] and there could be a fruitful coexistence between the ICC and such courts. As Kersten (2018) suggests, instead of regarding the ICC as being in opposition to such courts or in zero-sum terms, it would be useful to view them as elements in a network of international criminal justice. On the other hand, there were flaws in the first generation of hybrid courts, and there is no guarantee that a second generation will overcome the weaknesses (Hobbs 2018; Ottendoerfer 2018).

In any case, the ICC is likely to retain a pivotal position in the network of international criminal justice, but its current fraught relationships in Africa suggest that it has failed to navigate the problematic path between its judicial and political role. In principle, it could do much to enhance its legitimacy there and elsewhere by taking a more even-handed approach and addressing the crimes for which major Western powers and their allies are responsible. A step in this direction has been taken with preliminary examinations into alleged crimes against humanity and war crimes in Afghanistan. In a statement on 3 November 2017, the chief prosecutor, Fatou Bensouda, announced that she was taking this to the next stage by calling for an investigation. This could include possible war crimes of torture carried out by US military forces and the CIA, as well as the crimes committed by the Taliban. There are currently also

---

[3] In particular, the Extraordinary African Chambers was established by Senegal and the African Union in 2013 to prosecute international crimes committed in Chad during the presidency of Hissène Habré, who was subsequently convicted and sentenced to life imprisonment; a Special Criminal Court in the Central African Republic was expected to start its investigations in 2018; and the Kosovo Relocated Specialist Judicial Institution, which closely resembles a hybrid court, began functioning in 2016 to investigate crimes perpetrated between January 1998 and December 2000. This was set up to investigate crimes allegedly perpetrated by the victors of the war in Kosovo, whose members were seen as war heroes, leading to a political crisis and uncertainty about its future.

examinations into alleged war crimes committed by the UK in the Iraq conflict and into alleged crimes in the occupied Palestinian territory and East Jerusalem. Should any of these proceed, there would probably be a wider normative impact, affecting overall evaluations of the ICC. However, given the constraints under which the Court operates, such developments may be unlikely. Furthermore, taking the Afghanistan case further could provoke a major crisis with the US, as demonstrated in September 2018 when the US national security adviser, John Bolton, threatened sanctions if the ICC formally opened investigations on Afghanistan or pursued an inquiry into Israel. Any withdrawal of co-operation by the US could mean a serious reduction in the effectiveness of the Court. It will therefore need to juggle extremely skilfully between the dangers of being widely viewed as a partisan actor and jeopardising the support of the US on which it has depended.

Overall the international criminal justice 'network' has been important in helping to define and proscribe the most serious mass atrocity crimes, and it has had a positive impact in some situations. However, it can never be more than a limited element within TJ, and, as shown in the next chapter, it can sometimes have negative effects or be incompatible with other initiatives, particularly at local level. There is also a need for international actors to engage in more sustained and broader projects that go beyond counting the number of indictments and convictions and the length of sentences (Subotić 2009: 192).

Concluding Remarks

This chapter began by considering the challenge posed to TJ by the growing demand for proof of its effectiveness, which initiated the move towards evaluation. This was, no doubt, a necessary pressure on a field that had often rested largely on normative assumptions and faith about its effects. Since the early years of the current century, TJ has thus constantly sought to justify itself as 'evidence-based', and, as demonstrated in a penetrating overview, there is a continuing need for caution about exaggerated claims of success (Macdonald 2015). As we have seen, evaluation can take many forms.

Quantitative methods certainly have an important role, but they can also lead to attempts to measure the immeasurable and to force practitioners into ticking boxes in order to meet the demands of funders. In the allied context of peacebuilding, Reina Neufeldt has encapsulated two contrasting ontological universes that are also apparent in discussions of evaluation in TJ. One universe is inhabited by 'frameworkers', whose outlook is based on linear, cause–effect thinking or causal chains, and the other by 'complex circlers' using a more elliptical method, who tend to be relationship-focused and have an accompanying desire to be flexible and responsive to each situation (Neufeldt 2007; also cited in Dancy 2010). Neufeldt aspired to bring them together through a theory of change (2007: 16), but there is surely also a need to recognise the differences between the two outlooks. The problem is that the combination of positivist social science, seeking predictability and universal lessons, and donor pressure for quantitative evaluation often tends to squeeze out qualitative and ethically inspired approaches. As this chapter has shown, much highly valuable work in TJ has been based on such approaches, and, as Einstein purportedly said, 'not everything that can be counted counts and not everything that counts can be counted' (quoted ibid.: 6).

4

Specific Perspectives on Transitional Justice

The previous chapter considered evaluation generally and then examined the mechanisms of truth commissions and international criminal justice. However, TJ can also be evaluated from a variety of other angles, individually or together, and this chapter deals with just two of them – those that are 'victim-centred' and those informed by feminist and gendered perspectives. These touch on, and overlap with, other approaches, including viewing TJ through the lenses of ethnicity, class and inequality, or economic development. The discussion therefore seeks to illuminate some issues that transcend the two topics analysed here.

Victim Perspectives

TJ has constantly insisted that the interests of victims are integral to its goals, but this concern has not always been central in practice. Until the early twenty-first century, the key preoccupations were with securing effective transitions from repressive regimes or violent conflict, and the plight of victims was subsumed within these general goals (García-Godos 2016: 350–1). Since then, 'victim-centred' TJ has become a mantra, but it remains highly uncertain how far this is actually achieved – and, more fundamentally, it is debatable what it means. This section will explore such issues.

Although the families of the 'disappeared' played a major role in initiating the trials in Latin America, victims and survivors often seemed to be overlooked. For example, the International Criminal Tribunals for Rwanda and former Yugoslavia had no significant powers to deal with reparations, and there were criticisms of both institutions concerning their treatment of victims during the trials. Truth commissions have always been avowedly victim-centred – indeed, the South African Truth and Reconciliation Commission highlighted this aspect – but there have also been numerous complaints about their procedures (McEvoy and McConnachie 2013: 490–4). However, continuing mobilisation by victims and increasing international legal recognition of the right to reparations gradually changed the way that policy-makers conceived of TJ – at least in theory. As Pablo de Greiff put it in his first report to the UN as Special Rapporteur in 2012, none of the professed goals of TJ 'can happen effectively with victims as the key without their meaningful participation' (UN 2012a).

The ICC incorporated recognition of victims' rights, although it was left to the individual chambers to decide how to implement this commitment. Following this decision, there was a more general expectation that international criminal courts would allow victims to participate in some way, and the Extraordinary Chambers in the Courts of Cambodia went further by allowing victims similar rights to those of the defence and prosecution, including participation by supporting the prosecution. However, in both cases, the result has been confusion and dissatisfaction. The ICC enabled victims to participate in ways beyond those specified in the relevant Article (Article 68 [3]), which is extremely vague. This led to inconsistent practices and, from 2008 onwards, moves to curtail individual rights in favour of collective victim participation. The Extraordinary Chambers in the Courts of Cambodia increasingly moved to a similar position between 2008 and 2010, but in a way that caused still greater dissatisfaction because it constituted a reversal of an earlier policy that had allowed civil parties to participate in all criminal proceedings, including the investigative stage (Taylor 2014: 8–11).

More generally, there has been a lack of clarity, or unrealistic expectations, as to what victim participation was intended to achieve, both for the individuals themselves and for wider societal goals. Research on the *gacaca* courts in Rwanda and the Truth and Reconciliation Commission in South Africa suggests that the process of engaging in 'truth-telling' has been physically and emotionally damaging (Brounéus 2010 and Picker 2005, cited in Taylor 2014: 18–19; Ross 2010). In relation to both TCs and the courts, there were also feelings of disappointment that expectations had been raised without benefits being delivered. Taking on the status of a victim in court proceedings can lead to a feeling of being degraded (Mohan 2009: 768, cited in Taylor 2014: 19). Those who testify either to courts or to TCs have concerns about their safety, both in physical terms and in the possibility of social ostracism. Some may also feel that they are supposed to conform to a particular version of events with which they may not agree. Tutu's vision of the commission as a way of promoting reconciliation through forgiveness could alienate those who did not comply with this narrative (Madlingozi 2010: 215), and non-compliance with a dominant 'story' could be equally problematic in many other contexts (Taylor 2014: 34). Furthermore, divisions can be created between different kinds of victim, particularly if some are apparently regarded as more 'worthy' than others, as discussed further later.

This is not to suggest that victims' participation in TC and court processes is without value or to endorse the highly critical view that TJ experts (or 'entrepreneurs') have regarded themselves as ordained to teach, civilise and rescue helpless victims, 'stealing the pain of others', in order to reinstall First Worlders as morally and racially superior to them (Madlingozi 2010: 211, quoting Razack 2007). This form of cynical manipulation may sometimes exist, but in general TJ practitioners and theorists have no doubt been sincere in their view that the involvement of victims is valuable. And victim evidence has certainly contributed to knowledge about, and recognition of, past crimes and atrocities, with the telling of personal stories often having a major impact. Communicating some sense of victims' priorities about such issues as reparations contributed to raising the profile of this demand, and participation in formal TCs may also generate other, more accessible forms of truth-telling and civil society activity, as discussed in the previous chapter in relation to the Fambul Tok system in Sierra Leone. Some of the disappointment experienced by victim participants could be mitigated by comparatively minor reforms – for example, more training and outreach work about the processes; more follow-up and support for participants; greater sensitivity about how to reduce the stress of testifying; and providing a variety of means of giving evidence (Taylor 2014: 32–5). Yet even an improved process would be 'victim-centred' only in a restricted sense, both because of the limited number of people involved and because the institutions of TJ do not necessarily accord with the priorities and needs of affected communities.

'The Initiative for Vulnerable Populations' at the Human Rights Center in Berkeley, California, which carried out large-scale attitudinal surveys in order to develop more effective TJ programmes, demonstrated this. Some of the first surveys focused on attitudes towards types of justice and judicial mechanisms in Bosnia and Herzegovina, Croatia, Rwanda, Uganda and Iraq, and particular attention was paid to the differences between local responses and the mechanisms put in place at national or international level. The findings were specific for each country, but some of the authors suggested that the results posed several major challenges for TJ. In particular, they noted that legal justice might not be a high priority or desired at all, and that the primacy of Western legal systems and assumptions needed to be reviewed. They also highlighted the fact that the emphasis on international justice could sabotage both local democratic construction and the needs and desires of victims, who themselves had diverse notions of justice. Above all, they pointed out that many steps might be taken to rebuild societies and that there was as yet no clear understanding of which steps were the most critical – or, indeed, whether there was any universally valid programme (Fletcher et al. 2010: 47).

These criticisms implied a vast gap between the priorities of affected populations and the dominant approaches of TJ, and later attitudinal surveys demonstrated rather similar results, including further work in Uganda, as well as in the Democratic Republic of Congo, the Central African Republic, Liberia and Cambodia. For example, a survey was carried out in Northern Uganda in 2010, five years after the Lord's Resistance Army withdrew its forces from the area. The findings add substance to criticisms of the ICC discussed in the previous chapter. In this survey, some of the questions reflected the post-conflict context by including more questions about development and reconstruction. Some attitudes had changed, demonstrating that respondents felt far safer than previously. This meant that their priorities had shifted to basic needs, with 28 per cent highlighting food, 19 per cent agriculture, 15 per cent education, and 13 per cent healthcare. Almost all respondents (97 per cent) said that reparations should be granted to victims, usually because they were poor and needed support (49 per cent), but also as a form of acknowledgement or recognition of their suffering (24 per cent) and to help them forget (19 per cent). There were mixed views about both the formal justice system and TJ mechanisms in general. The report therefore recommended that both the government of Uganda and the international community needed to meet the priorities of the survey respondents by a multipronged strategy promoting peacebuilding, socioeconomic development, justice and poverty reduction in the north; that the population must become more involved in the development and implementation of recovery efforts; and that there needed to be a reparation programme that was both realistic and addressed the needs of the survivors, giving them ownership of, and participation in, such efforts (Pham and Vinck 2010). Such policies were very far removed from contemporary practice.

The findings of a study in a conflict-dominated zone in the east of the Democratic Republic of Congo were generally similar, but still more dramatic. In a situation of continuing fear and violence, issues of justice, reintegration and reconciliation were not priorities, with only 2.3 per cent mentioning justice, 1.6 per cent advocating the arrest of those responsible for violence, and 1.3 per cent favouring both punishment and reconciliation (Vinck and Pham 2008: 402–3). In theory, there had been a Truth and Reconciliation Commission in the country from 2003 to 2007, but this failed to hear a single case and included commissioners from the belligerent parties. Of greater significance, although Thomas Lubanga had been arrested in 2006, only 26.6 per cent of respondents had heard of the ICC. Peace (50.5 per cent) and security (34.1 per cent) were the issues that were most frequently mentioned, followed by livelihood concerns, including financial assistance (26.8 per cent), education (26.4 per cent) and food and water (25.8 per cent). The authors concluded that TJ mechanisms needed to be part of a broader set of policies for socioeconomic development and reconciliation – again measures that were wholly absent.

Perhaps the greatest gap of all between victims' priorities and TJ mechanisms was revealed in the survey on Cambodia published in 2009. This was based on interviews of 1,000 Cambodians of at least eighteen years of age carried out in September–October 2008. These took place after the Extraordinary Chambers in the Courts of Cambodia finally became active, as there had been nine arrests of Khmer Rouge leaders during the previous year (although the trials had not yet begun). Sixty-nine per cent of respondents had lived under the Khmer Rouge regime, while 31 per cent were born after its overthrow; 93 per cent of the first group regarded themselves as victims; but even 51 per cent of those born later thought of themselves in this way.

The overwhelming majority of the survivors reported having experienced starvation or a lack of food, a lack of shelter, the theft or destruction of their personal property, and forced labour and evacuation. Approximately one in four respondents reported having been tortured; nearly one in three witnessed torture and over one in five saw killings (Pham et al. 2009). With these personal experiences of abuse and atrocities, a high level of support for the Extraordinary Chambers as the primary mechanism of TJ in Cambodia might be expected. Yet over 80 per cent of respondents said that their priorities were jobs, followed by services to meet basic needs. When asked what the priorities of the government should be, only 2 per cent mentioned justice, and the main preoccupations were the economy and infrastructure development. Over 75 per cent thought it more important to focus on the problems that people faced in their daily lives than to address crimes committed in the past; 39 per cent had no knowledge of the Extraordinary Chambers and 46 per cent had only limited knowledge. Finally, the vast majority (88 per cent) thought that reparations should be provided, and 68 per cent argued that they should be given to the community as a whole; many people mentioned that these should be in a form that affected daily lives – for example, through social services and infrastructure development.

These attitudes need to be contextualised, for the government had constantly sabotaged efforts at TJ, encouraging people to concentrate on the present rather than the past. Nevertheless, there could scarcely be a greater disjuncture between the stated priorities of the majority of the population (most of whom regarded themselves as victims) and the formal TJ processes. More generally, these mass attitudinal surveys revealed the gulf between the priorities of conventional TJ and those of vulnerable communities in many areas affected by violence and atrocities. Of course, attitudes may evolve rapidly, and victims are not homogeneous but consist of multiple constituencies, so such surveys need to be coupled with qualitative evidence (Shaw and

Waldorf 2010: 20). Much of this has been derived from other studies.

A recent work on grassroots activism by families of the disappeared in Lebanon, Cyprus, South Africa and Chile has demonstrated the continuing significance of bereaved relatives in the evolution of TJ, following the path set by their predecessors in Argentina (Kovras 2017). A key aspect of this study is its refutation of any notion of victims as passive objects of policies defined from above. It argues that, without the mobilised families demanding to know what happened to their loved ones and uncovering the truth, legal processes and TCs may not have developed (ibid.: 233–4). The continuing grassroots activism by relatives of the disappeared also enlarged the conceptualisation of TJ to encompass additional mechanisms. The way in which this has occurred in relation to the development of reparations, including collective and symbolic forms such as memori-alisation, has already been considered, but Kovras draws attention to the development of forensic sciences in exhuma-tions so as to uncover evidence about burials and violence as a further contribution to families' search for the truth about the past (ibid.: 6).

Such insights also provide a valuable corrective to any idea that TJ should be regarded as confined to either discrete measures or specific temporal forms: while relatives may be constrained in one situation or period by 'institution-alised silence' or amnesty laws, so that even humanitarian exhumations and identification of the dead require activism, the boundaries may shift later. Thus at the time of the transition in Chile it was difficult to talk about the past at all, but after 1998 the climate gradually changed. Families of the disappeared now played a catalytic role in establishing truth recovery mechanisms that documented the condi-tions behind the disappearances, leading to prosecutions and the gradual erosion of the amnesty laws, as was also the case in Argentina and Guatemala (Kovras 2017: 6–8, 234–7). Yet in some situations, rather than victims' families gradually pushing forward the TJ process, there may be sharp contradictions between their priorities and those of national and international policy-makers, as Simon Robins has shown in his studies of Nepal and Timor-Leste.

This research was carried out in extended interviews with families of the 'disappeared' – during the civil war of 1996–2006 in Nepal and during the independence struggle with Indonesia from 1975 to 1999 in Timor-Leste (Robins 2011, 2012). Although the circumstances differed, Robins argues that, in both cases, existing approaches to TJ were misconceived because they were based primarily on practices and concepts devised by the international TJ community. These were completely inappropriate for poor societies and, in particular, for the most affected communities within them. In Nepal, Robins sought to examine this with particular reference to the families of the 1,200 'disappeared' following the civil war, and in Timor-Leste the research was based on a list of 2,452 missing people. In both cases, the majority of the victims were rural, poor and illiterate, unfamiliar with the discourse of rights and far more likely to talk of urgent daily needs. This confirms the findings in the surveys of attitudes outlined above but goes further in emphasising the differences within a single country, demonstrating that needs may be very local (as also shown in the discussion of traditional informal justice systems in chapter 2). In particular, there was a considerable difference between the city dwellers and rural people and between those in the capital and those outside it (Robins 2013).

In general, though, the priorities were to achieve certainty about the fate of the disappeared and to have their bodies, to secure economic support and recognition of their situation, and to have an acknowledgement by the authorities of what happened. Still more notably, conventional TJ failed to engage with the belief systems of traditional rural communities rooted in extended family relationships. For example, almost all the missing in both societies were men, but the female survivors then faced particular problems, not only as a result of economic deprivation but also because of social and cultural attitudes. Wives may not want to dress as widows because they refuse to accept that their husbands are dead, but this can then lead to discrimination and stigma.

Conventional TJ might simply regard the fact of disappearance as signifying a loss for which some kind of reparations will be appropriate (if never adequate), but this fails to capture the spiritual dimensions of the problems, where the most important cultural element is the performance of rituals that are only possible when there is a certainty of death. The relevant truth for the survivors is not a public truth about the past, as in mainstream TJ, but this more personal truth; and the collective healing is not through a TC, but through the traditional rituals. The problem, in Robins's view, is not simply that the affected communities do not share the discourse of human rights but that this concept undermines them and their own possibility of agency. The language of human rights suggests that governments and law are significant and bring about change, but many victims believe that traditional customs and practices define the world, and concepts favoured by conventional TJ entail their being treated as objects rather than subjects (Robins 2013).

Overall, this 'victim-centred' perspective offers a critical evaluation of TJ, not only in Nepal and Timor-Leste but generally. It privileges everyday understandings and priorities in the lives of victims and argues that current practices are embedded in a global approach, which necessarily fails to engage with local understandings constructed through historical and cultural specificity. This means that conventional TJ offers both an insufficient range of measures and, simultaneously, ignores the available community resources for solutions to injustice and violence. For Robins also argues that the victims have agency to bring about change in opposition to the existing elite-driven mechanisms rather than acquiescing in the current mechanisms. Of course, it is not only families of the 'disappeared' who have challenged official processes that appear to turn victims into passive 'objects' of TJ, as shown in one further example: the Khulumani in South Africa.

This organisation (meaning 'Speak Out') was created in order to facilitate the participation of victims and survivors in the Truth and Reconciliation Commission. But many members soon felt that this betrayed them, since promises regarding reparations and truth recovery were never met and they were urged to forgive perpetrators and beneficiaries of the apartheid system who showed no remorse (Madlingozi 2010: 214–15). Khulumani, which claimed a membership of more than 100,000 by 2016, has always aspired to be a 'bottom-up', non-hierarchical movement, organised by victims and survivors themselves (www.khulumani.net/). Its work falls into three main phases: the initial stage supported victims in engaging with the formal process; a second phase (from 1998 to 2006) consisted of mobilisation and advocacy around reparations issues; and a third, ongoing phase involves a range of activities, including agricultural and entrepreneurial projects and exerting pressure on the South African government to meet its unfulfilled commitments (Madlingozi 2010: 216–18).

A continuing aspect of Khulumani's work has been its attempt to secure reparations for economic aspects of apartheid, including in a high-profile, but thus far unsuccessful, case against Barclays Bank and several other transnational companies, which was heard in a New York Court in 2004. In 2012 this led General Motors to settle with a symbolic payment of $1.5 million without admitting wrongdoing. But a central objective of the organisation is to build a social movement that will enable the transformation and empowerment of victims through their own actions. As Vasuki Nesiah has noted, this means that the failure of the court case should not lead to a negative evaluation of the work of Khulumani because this international legal action may still have contributed to victim empowerment by extending the reach of the processes of the Truth and Reconciliation Commission beyond the expectations or plans of its architects (Nesiah 2016: 23).

This ties in with a more general conception of victims who define their own priorities, develop their own agency and shape policies. In this perspective, the international role might be one of support, advocacy and facilitation rather than an attempt to reconcile affected peoples with existing TJ policies and practices. A community activist in Northern Uganda has encapsulated the difference in approach. He reported that large NGOs which worked in the area claimed that local people did not want an amnesty and favoured the ICC. In fact, he argued, it was the NGOs that had these priorities, while the community 'saw the soldiers in the LRA [Lord's Resistance Army] as victims, as their children' (quoted in McEvoy and McConnachie 2013: 499). More generally, the core of a 'bottom-up' participatory approach to victim-centred TJ has been identified as suggesting that this requires a response to the explicit needs of victims, as defined by the victims themselves. This does not imply that all the goals of the process should be made subservient to the agenda of the victims, but it does necessitate either broad consultation with them or that they and their representatives are engaged at all levels of planning and implementation. The effectiveness of the process could then be measured in terms of its ability to address victims' needs (Robins 2011: 77). In my view, this conception enhances those of more conventional approaches in many important ways. However, there are also some problems in notions of victim-centred justice.

Representing situations in terms of a dichotomy between perpetrators and victims has been the way in which TJ has tended to be framed, and there are certainly situations in which this may seem appropriate. For example, the genocide in Guatemala was aimed primarily at the indigenous community and was carried out by massacres orchestrated from above. Similarly, if one takes a particular set of victims, such as the disappeared, the category appears relatively straightforward. But there are many situations in which perpetrators may also be victims, perhaps because their superiors intimidated them with threats to their own lives or because their opponents targeted them. Conventional TJ has tended to prefer categories of 'guilty' and 'innocent'.

Concessions may be made to certain groups regarded as vulnerable, such as child soldiers, as in the case that opened 2016 in the ICC, when Dominic Ongwen, a former commander of the Lord's Resistance Army, claimed that he had been acting under duress. However, making exceptions for child soldiers, and also sometimes women combatants, still preserves the distinction between the guilty and the innocent that TJ has generally wished to uphold (McEvoy and McConnachie 2013: 500). Yet, as discussed in chapter 1, simply dividing people into two categories may also divert attention from structural explanations of violence and atrocities, and there are many situations in which a binary division between (guilty) perpetrators and (innocent) victims may be unhelpful in understanding and addressing the past.

There are also situations, discussed in previous chapters, in which victimhood may be used politically in negative ways. For example, following the end of the violent conflict in Peru between state forces and the Shining Path, the government deliberately created the category of 'innocent' victims, which the 2005 Reparations Law reinforced by excluding members of subversive organisations from being potential beneficiaries (Theidon 2010: 105). In fact, many people in indigenous rural communities had been victims of repression by the state rather than by Shining Path and had some sympathy with the latter organisation. However, they now sought to reconstruct their own histories, both because the state used anti-terrorist rhetoric to stifle dissent and because only 'innocent victims' could receive reparations. This categorisation therefore reinforced pre-existing divisions between communities, failed to bring about reconciliation and created resentful silences (ibid.: 109–10). The narrative of victims and terrorists was used to avoid grappling with difficult questions – such as whether the orphans of Shining Path members who were murdered were entitled to reparations (Malca 2015: 120).

Similarly, instead of focusing equally on all the victims, the current regime in Rwanda has treated the genocide as if it was perpetrated solely against Tutsis, thereby relegating massacred Hutus to a position of secondary importance, and this has also been the case in the former Yugoslavia, where all the communities claim victimhood. More generally, 'victim-centred' justice can be exploited for various agendas, including a demand for revenge and retribution or in an attempt to favour some communities or individuals at the expense of others.

While victims' groups and their external supporters may therefore play a crucial role in campaigning and mobilising support for justice, this does not mean either that the demands of each group or the communities in which they are based should be the *exclusive* focus of TJ, or that their situation will necessarily always be the most effectively remedied in this way. This is partly because the needs and demands of groups or areas may be particular and local and cannot simply be aggregated into an optimum national solution, and also because some victims may constitute themselves as more worthy than others. Sometimes the leaders of victim communities may also be based on hierarchies of gender, ethnicity or political affiliation, which policy-makers could legitimately refuse to respect (Nesiah 2016: 25). There may even be complex contradictions between the priorities of the families of the disappeared, who favour the continuation of amnesties so that perpetrators might help locate bodies or mass graves, and national priorities favouring forms of retributive justice, as was the case in Colombia in the aftermath of the Justice and Peace Law in 2005 (Kovras 2017: 243). As McEvoy and McConnachie suggest, victims and victims' organisations, rather than simply being accepted in an uncritical way, should be subject to the same level of scrutiny to be applied to all other relevant actors (2013: 505). While victim-centred TJ is undoubtedly important, the goal is surely to seek overall justice, as discussed in the final chapter.

Feminist and Gendered Perspectives

Feminism is diverse and contested, and there have been many debates as to whether it has any specific methodological and epistemological approach (Doucet and Mauthner 2007). This section is based on the view that feminism raises fundamental questions about gendered stereotypes, social roles, and power relationships more generally and follows the approach that holds that feminist research depends less on the method used than how it is used and for what purposes (Westmarland 2001, citing Kelly et al. 1992: 150). In relation to TJ, this suggests that feminist and gendered perspectives *should* make a difference as to how the subject is conceived and practised, opening up areas that have been hidden by more conventional analyses and pointing to forms of social and political organisation in which justice may be realised in new ways.

During the early phase of TJ, it was relatively easy for feminists to agree on one notable feature in its theory and practice: the virtual absence of a gender dimension or gender sensitivity. Feminist contributions therefore tended to emphasise the necessity to transform this absence by 'presence' – that is, by ensuring that women were fully repre-sented in the decision-making, institutions and procedures of TJ. Of equal importance was the demand for recognition of the fact that women are adversely affected by repressive regimes and violent conflict in specific ways that would not be addressed unless they played an active role in defining and rectifying these 'harms'. But this apparently simple point masks layers of complexity and controversy.

TJ emerged from the spheres of law and human rights, but these tended to be based in gender-neutral or androgynous assumptions, either with the virtual occlusion of gendered crime or an understatement of its significance. For example, rape was not categorised as a 'grave breach' of the Geneva Conventions of 1949, making it a crime of lesser consequence, subject only to domestic jurisdiction (Ní Aoláin 2000: 68). A key focus for feminist demands has therefore been to ensure that crimes of sexual violence are recognised and addressed, and feminist pressure led to developments in international criminal law. Other forms of TJ, such as TCs, evolved in a similar way. Thus, while the early TCs in Argentina and

Chile were 'gender neutral', there was a gradual advance, and later TCs have interpreted their terms of reference in such a way as to address sexual violence; those in Haiti, Sierra Leone and East Timor/Timor-Leste explicitly incorporated these dimensions into their mandates. Following important landmarks, such as Resolution 1325 at the UN on 'Women, Peace and Security', there was also an increasing tendency for peace settlements formally to recognise the importance of the participation of women, including in TJ mechanisms (Bell and O'Rourke 2007: 28–34). Nevertheless, a review of thirty-one major peace processes between 1992 and 2011 by the UN Entity for Gender Equality and Empowerment of Women still showed that only 4 per cent of the signatories were women (UN 2012b).

Feminist critiques of the slow pace of change have raised both empirical and conceptual questions. In her examination of the ICC, for example, Louise Chappell has argued that, despite an inbuilt gender sensitivity, its record in practice has been inconsistent and its possibilities of bringing about gendered TJ in future will depend upon continuing support, pressure and criticisms, including by NGOs (Chappell 2012: 46–54). More generally, in judicial settings, selective choices are always made about upholding particular norms, resulting in a gap in enforcement, which has been particularly marked in cases that concern female populations in the context of TJ (Ní Aoláin 2012a: 64–80). There have also been important critiques of the failure of courts to provide a supportive forum for women to recount their experiences (Mertus 2004). But these points are related to wider issues about law. Many have argued that this privileges a 'male view of the universe', with an emphasis on a public/private distinction, 'leaving the private sphere of the individual untouched' (Charlesworth 1994: 65; 1999: 387, quoted in Ní Aoláin 2012b: 210). More generally, it has been widely agreed that international laws have tended to privilege particular kinds of harm that focus on physical abuse, rather than on the social, economic and cultural forms of discrimination and oppression that constitute much of the daily reality of women's lives. These points also apply to other forms of TJ, with the argument that a feminist perspective needs to tackle multiple and inter-related forms of 'harm', theorised by Catherine O'Rourke as a gendered 'web of harms' (O'Rourke 2013: 37–8).

Yet feminist evaluations of TJ also have to grapple with difficult conceptual dilemmas. Gender-based sexual violence has clearly been a source of oppression and suffering, and this is often particularly pronounced in repressive regimes and violent conflict. The urgent need to address this has inevitably formed an important element in feminist approaches to TJ. But there are also dangers of oversimplification, for the experience of gender-based sexual violence may vary according to class, region, religion and status, and there are male and transgender victims as well. Feminists have sought to avoid an exclusive focus on this form of violence because it can reinforce the stereotype of women as victims in need of protection rather than as active political participants capable of exerting agency in bringing about social transformation. Furthermore, an undue emphasis on sexual violence may imply that this is entirely separate from all other features of society rather than being embedded in deeper socioeconomic structures and patriarchal attitudes. Feminist perspectives therefore draw attention to gender-based sexual violence as just one element in the collective interests of women in transitional situations, along with other gendered problems – for example, in their position as refugees, dependency on aid, lack of equal access to social and economic goods, exclusion from political processes and lower legal status (Ní Aoláin 2012b: 207).

The relationships between gender, violence and transitional justice also depend on different contexts and sometimes take forms that are not immediately obvious. For example, during the revolutionary/civil war periods, there were female fighters in the Maoist forces in Nepal and FARC in Colombia, thereby apparently calling into question the familiar assumptions of female passivity and victimhood. Following the ending of the civil war, despite some rhetoric of gender equality, Nepal quickly reverted to a traditional society in which women occupied a very subordinate position. In Colombia the peace settlement included several aspects that specifically sought to advance the role of women, but here, too, the civil war had privileged a violent form of masculinity that was reflected in the TJ mechanisms, which were based on a 'gender-blind' conception of citizenship. In an evaluation of the situation (written before the peace settlement was instituted), Catherine O'Rourke thus argued that a truly transitional form of justice for all victims would involve disarming the form of masculinity that upholds violence in social relations in peace as well as war (O'Rourke 2012: 150–5, 157). Shana Tabak also emphasised the importance of countering false dichotomies in TJ, highlighting the need both to work specifically with men and to recognise the multiplicity of roles that may be played by individuals, while tackling the dominant gender dynamics that perpetuate conflict (Tabak 2011: 162–3). And this is rather similar in the South African context, where both repression and violence fostered an aggressive form of masculinity that continued after the end of apartheid (Sigsworth and Valji 2012: 121–9).

But evaluation of each situation requires an informed gender-sensitive analysis, which is not always present. In Liberia, for example, the TC stressed the plight of women as victims of violent attacks but, because of its own underlying assumptions about gender, failed to point out that at least a third of the combatants were young women (Buckley-Zistel and Zolkos 2012: 11). Incorporating such points into an overall feminist viewpoint often involves a broad notion of transitional justice in which some fundamental assumptions are questioned. In particular, since the subordinate situation of women and gender-based sexual violence generally pre-date an authoritarian regime or civil war and continue after its termination, feminist theory is often critical of any simple idea of 'transition'. Yet there are nuances here too. As Aisling Swaine has demonstrated in a comparative study of Northern Ireland, Liberia and Timor-Leste, there are continuities but also significant differences in the form and scale of violence in the situations before, during and after conflict, and the interrelationships between these need to be addressed in TJ (Swaine 2018). Feminist analysis also questions conventional notions of 'justice' and strives to define multidimensional concepts by including full gender equality while simultaneously valuing difference (Bell and O'Rourke 2007).

Feminist critiques and evaluations therefore tend to be based on transformative goals, but this does not mean that there is any agreed position. For example, critical feminist approaches to TJ have often emphasised the importance of using reparations to help facilitate socioeconomic transformation, but Margaret Urban Walker has rejected this suggestion. While acknowledging that fundamental transformation might be a proper goal for TJ, she argues that individuals' right to claim accountability and repair for violations should not be subordinated to the pursuit of systemic and structural change (Walker 2016). And Catherine O'Rourke has used her 'web of harms' to explore the relationship between the 'public' and 'private' in unusual ways, maintaining that that violent conflict and political repression exacerbate and alter the nominally 'private' harms of violence against women. She argues that action needs to be taken against all gendered harms, but that this does not mean that the private and public should be conflated.

O'Rourke has made a further contribution that raises very important issues. While taking a critical approach to TJ, she nevertheless suggests that an emphasis solely on negative outcomes can lead to a conclusion that there are immutable patriarchies and that women are inevitably in a position of marginality, exclusion and powerlessness. In her view, the task is to explain why some transitions are better for women than others and to recognise that participation and inclusion can affect outcomes positively (O'Rourke 2013: 8, 248). Her study focuses on the differing situations in Chile, Colombia and Northern Ireland and traces the ways in which evolving international norms had a partially beneficial impact, although this remained very limited in relation to the whole range of private and public harms.

O'Rourke's case studies were in self-reliant states in which there was relatively little international involvement in the TJ processes, and, as she noted, the situation was quite different in states where international intervention had taken place. For, in these contexts, international actors might turn to local women's organisations to legitimise external involvement, but local elites often subsequently tend to manipulate or resist the official processes. This meant that framing the operation of TJ in terms of women's equality and human rights might be very short term (O'Rourke 2013: 13, 246). This is clearly often true, but outcomes can vary according to the specific local political dynamics here too, as shown in the following discussion of two pairs of comparatively weak states – first Sierra Leone and Timor-Leste and then Cambodia and Rwanda.

Sierra Leone is one of the poorest countries in the world, ranked at 184 (out of 189) in the human development statistical update for 2018 (in the 'low' category), while Timor-Leste was ranked at 132 (in the 'medium' category). There were appalling levels of gender-based sexual violence during the Sierra Leonean civil war and in East Timor/Timor-Leste during the long period of Indonesian occupation and final struggle for independence. Both then incorporated relatively advanced aspects of gender equality into their systems of TJ, with international actors playing a key role. In Sierra Leone, both the Special Court and the Truth and Reconciliation Commission highlighted gender, and the latter was mandated to pay special attention to the subject of sexual abuse (Teale 2009). Under the UN Transitional Administration, the Commission for Reception, Truth and Reconciliation also developed quite advanced gender-inclusive strategies in East Timor/Timor-Leste. Its gender unit worked actively to ensure that women's experiences were recorded; it commissioned additional oral histories so that the collective public memory included the experiences of women and implemented training programmes to increase their political engagement (Democratic Progress Institute 2015: 32–3; Valji 2012). However, in confirmation of the point about internationally dominated gender policies tending to have disappointing long-term results in such contexts, neither Sierra Leone nor Timor-Leste has changed dramatically in the post-transition periods. Yet it would be simplistic either to assume inevitability or to ignore the specificities of each situation.

In Sierra Leone, the TJ processes led to extensive domestic legislation, and the attention paid to sexual violence also resulted in far more public discourse about gender inequality in general. Yet this did not lead to measurable change in gender-based violence, partly because of a continuing lack of enforcement and accountability for such crimes and perhaps also because men felt threatened by the new norms and responded with still greater gender-based violence. Moreover, the general position of women and girls has remained deeply unequal (Oosterveld 2015: 130–43). One problem was that the women's movement was unable to maintain its earlier impetus in the immediate aftermath of the war. Demands for equal access to political representation were reduced, but by 2014 even the lower target had not been achieved because of resistance by male politicians, who constituted nearly 88 per cent of MPs, and the minority of women in parliament put party loyalty above any collective gender interest (Abdullah 2014). While a high percentage of women MPs may not always lead to gains for women, their absence makes it less likely that entrenched inequalities and discrimination will be tackled.

Part of the failure also suggests that the women's movement had insufficient allies in the government to ensure progress, but this requires focusing at least as much on the traditional structures at local level as on the central institutions (Castillejo 2009). However, it should not be concluded that the position has been static, as, for example, demonstrated by work carried out in Kailahun (in the far east of the country, with a population of around 400,000) by the Kailahun Women in Governance Network, which supported women aspiring to political and electable positions in the 2013 elections. This showed considerable progress in increased opportunities for women's involvement in decision-making and in generally positive attitudes to female councillors, but also continuing intimidation and fears of sexual violence (Christian Aid 2015). This mixed record is also implied in that Sierra Leone's ranking at 150 in the Gender Inequality Index in the 2018 human development statistical update – thirty-four places above its general human development ranking.

Unlike Sierra Leone, Timor-Leste has experienced significant economic growth since gaining independence in 2002, benefiting from a strong oil sector that provided the state with funding for major improvements in social expenditure (World Bank 2018). Yet despite very substantial progress in such spheres as health and education, massive inequality between urban and rural areas remained, with no significant reduction in poverty alleviation between 2001 and 2011 and the vast majority of the poor (76 per cent) living in rural areas (Asian Development Bank 2014: 5). These inequalities have also had a major impact on the position of women, particularly in these areas. The Commission for Reception Truth and Reconciliation and its follow-up work certainly led to some progress, and there were signs of a continuing commitment to the promotion of equality for women, but the effectiveness of gender-inclusion policies was limited in practice (Porter 2012: 221–37). A gender quota law in 2006 meant that the country now has one of Asia's highest percentages of female MPs (38 per cent), and many women have gained from the social and economic advances and changes in the labour market. There has also been progress through the Penal Code in 2009, which provided gender equality in many spheres of life, and through the Law against Domestic Violence the following year. Yet domestic violence and maternal mortality remain high, employment is extremely unequal in gender terms, and there is very low female participation in local government (the most important level for rural women); almost all village and hamlet chiefs are male (98 per cent) (Asian Development Bank 2014: xvi).

Timor-Leste remains a patriarchal society, with cultural practices perpetuating gender inequality; despite rapid development leading to questioning of traditional norms, many of these remain entrenched (Asian Development Bank 2014: 6). There are also some particularly complex inter-actions between the period of conflict and the current situation that have made it difficult for an autonomous women's movement to play a clear role in assuring funda-mental changes. The resistance against Indonesia between 1975 and 1999 led to the emergence of a leadership based on a militarised masculinity, which continued to dominate the new society. There are also former women combatants who believed that it was impossible to fight for equal rights during the armed struggle, but who have subsequently found it difficult to demand fundamental changes since this would necessitate opposition to the men with whom they were closely allied in the past. Another crucial factor is that a number of customary practices – for example, those related to marriage (known as 'barlake'), which involve the subju-gation of women, remain embedded in Timorese indigenous culture. In order to address and change the situation, it will be necessary to engage more actively with these traditions (Niner 2017).

Despite the fact that Timor-Leste is now significantly wealthier than Sierra Leone, its record in relation to gender inequality may be worse. There was no ranking for it in the *Gender Inequality Index* in the human development statistics in 2018 because the data was not supplied, but in 2013 it was ranked at 118 out of 149 countries, and its position would have been lower – close to that of Papua New Guinea and Afghanistan (respectively ranked at 159 and 153 in the 2018 index) – had it not been for the relatively high participation of women in parliament. Both Sierra Leone and Timor-Leste thus have entrenched patriarchal systems, and feminist movements have been unable to secure sufficient purchase to bring about fundamental change in the post-transition societies. However, there are also obvious differences, both in the general functioning of the societies and in the traditions in which the systems' subordination and discrimination are anchored. Let us now turn to Rwanda and Cambodia, which have one common factor in their recent histories – horrific genocides.

There are vast differences in the ways in which the genocide was addressed in the two states, largely because in Rwanda the new Tutsi-led regime constituted a complete break from the previously Hutu-dominated system, while a major feature in Cambodia has been considerable continuity with the Khmer Rouge regime. The Rwandan government sought drastic and rapid action, but its counterparts in Cambodia tried to delay and undermine TJ of any kind, and only recently has there been any significant progress. The fact that forms of TJ were instituted immediately after the genocide in Rwanda and only haltingly, almost thirty years later, in Cambodia obviously also made a significant difference. But there were some similarities. Both were subject to international influences but took effective control of TJ, though in the case of Cambodia this consisted largely of seeking to subvert it, and both are authoritarian states.

Pre-genocide Cambodia was a highly traditional society in which women were normally totally dependent on men for their earnings and were mainly limited to the household. The family was a central feature of this society, underpinning the economic, cultural and religious institutions (Mam 2004, cited in Sankey 2016: 15). The Khmer Rouge regime was in total contrast to these traditions in three respects. Firstly, it was based on an ideology that sought to destroy the existing forms of social relationships and create a new system, consciously attempting to eliminate the family and replace it with loyalty to the collective leadership. Secondly, it established forced migration from cities in its aspiration to create an agrarian society, and this involved the deliberate separation of families. Thirdly, war conditions created a situation in which existing family structures broke down, and women took on roles that had previously been closed to them. In principle, the Khmer Rouge supported such changes and wanted to create a 'gender-blind' society in which social and cultural expressions of femininity were outlawed.

In fact, Khmer Rouge practices contradicted such theories in some of the most brutal ways imaginable. However, this was disguised by the fact that the Khmer Rouge had a law against rape which carried a possible penalty of execution for the perpetrator if discovered, and by the acknowledgement that there were 'arranged marriages' without making their nature explicit. In reality, rape and other forms of sexual violence were committed against women, and sexual enslavement was inflicted on both sexes. The 'arranged marriages' were a particularly brutal form of 'forced marriage' in which women were sometimes compelled to marry injured soldiers and were imprisoned or tortured if they refused. None of this was addressed by the post-genocide regime, and the claims of the Khmer Rouge regime were generally accepted internationally. Once the Extraordinary Chambers in the Courts of Cambodia finally began, progress on the issue of sexual violence was extremely slow, and a female international judge publicly stated in 2011 that the Khmer Rouge was one of the few criminal regimes in which gender-based violence did not comprise a major part of its behaviour (de Langis and Studzinsky 2012).

The situation is quite different in Rwanda. Women still suffer disproportionately in terms of poverty, inequality and marginalisation (Mageza-Barthel 2012: 185), and there are serious limitations in their autonomous political role. Major criticisms have also been made of the way in which gender-based violence was addressed in TJ. Under pressure from women's movements, rape and sexual violence were recognised as constituting the most serious form of crime in the early post-genocide period, but in 2008 the law was changed, meaning that such cases were dealt with in the *gacaca* rather than in conventional courts, apparently treating sexual violence as a lower category crime and carrying other disadvantages for the victims (Human Rights

Watch 2011: 111–18). Nevertheless, the situation of women is in marked contrast to that in Cambodia.

In the Hutu-dominated state, a women's movement had begun to develop in the mid-1980s, leading to some pressure on the government, which created a Ministry for the Promotion of Women and the Family in 1992 and appointed the first female prime minister in 1993 (Burnet 2008: 372–3). The assumption of power in 1994 by the Tutsi-dominated RPF injected far greater impetus into such advances. Women were appointed to high-profile positions in government, and a new ministry was created which, from 1998, organised elections for representative leadership among women at all levels of government and subsequently incorporated gender analysis into all policies and legislation (ibid.: 367–8). There was also a dramatic proliferation of autonomous women's organisations in the country, making them the most active sector of civil society between 1994 and 2003 (ibid.: 373–5). The new regime therefore precipitated major changes in the position of women, partly by deliberate 'top-down' policies, partly because the genocide itself created problems that urgently needed to be addressed, and partly because of pressure from women's movements. The convergence of these influences led to important early results, changing discriminatory property and land ownership laws (Democratic Progress Institute 2015: 24–5), partly because of demographic changes as a result of the greater number of deaths among men during the genocide (Burnet 2008: 383).

There are differing interpretations of the separate impact of the various influences in bringing about such changes. For example, Jenny Burnet takes an anthropological approach, focusing largely on women's lives and multiple influences on them (Burnet 2012: 219–21), while Rihanda Mageza-Barthel has explored the complex interactions between international norms and the domestic political role of both feminists and the ruling party (Mageza-Barthel 2015: 145–52). Some fortuitous factors also had an influence, such as the growing importance of women judges, initially because of the need to replace many of the male judges in the *gacaca* courts because of their involvement in the genocide (Ingelaere 2008: 48). Any explanation of the transformation must be multidimensional, but Rwanda now has the highest percentage of women MPs in the world, at 61.3 per cent, and 50 per cent of Supreme Court judges are women. This has led to a series of relevant laws, from the protection of children from violence in 2001 to an extensive Matrimonial Regimes Law in August 2016.

In Cambodia, in contrast, progress was very slow even after the issue of gender- and sexually based violence was finally put on the agenda of the Extraordinary Chambers. A German attorney, Silke Studzinsky, played a key role by recognising that 'organised marriage' was a euphemism for rape and sexual violence (Studzinsky 2012: 94–108). One case, which began in November 2011, led to the indictment of two senior former leaders for a series of crimes, including forced marriage. The Cambodian Women's Hearing on Sexual Violence under the Khmer Rouge in Phnom Penh in December 2011, where victims and witnesses and survivors testified about their experience of sexual violence, also had an impact. However, the following May, a briefing paper for the Special Representative of the UN Secretary-General on Sexual Violence still warned that the survivors of 'rampant sexual violence' were suffering in a 'culture of impunity that blames and stigmatizes the victim and allows perpetrators to go free' (de Langis and Studzinsky 2012), and the Extraordinary Chambers remained rather vague on rape outside marriage (Oosterveld and Sellers 2016: 348–50). There are also other gendered aspects of the genocide that have hardly been addressed, particularly in relation to the differential impact of the forced migration and the break-up of families on women and men, given the overwhelmingly female role in caring for the young and elderly in Cambodian society (Sankey 2016: 15–19).

The failures in tackling gendered aspects of the genocide are reflected in subsequent developments. Certainly, there have been some gains, as the government has been keen to highlight (Kingdom of Cambodia 2005), and there have been women's and other civil society movements in Cambodia (Marks and Naraharisetti 2013). There has also been some progress in enhancing the position of women in terms of occupying decision-making roles in society (UNDP 2014). But gender inequality remains deeply entrenched in the continuation of the patriarchal political and social culture. Before 2005, domestic violence was not illegal, and, although the law of that year was an important step forward, it remained ambiguous in key provisions and enforcement (CAMBOW 2007). A multi-country report for the UN in 2013 (Fulu et al. 2013, cited by Salvá 2016) found that more than 20 per cent of Cambodian men aged between eighteen and forty-nine admitted that they had committed rape, and 96.2 per cent of men and 98.5 per cent of women thought that a woman should obey her husband; 67 per cent of women believed that they should tolerate violence in order to maintain the family. The report, which also showed alarmingly high levels of violence in other countries in the region, demonstrated that the causes are complex. But it is surely relevant that the traditional codes of conduct such as the Chbab Srey (Women's Law) taught women and girls to serve men, instructing them to be quiet, submissive, deferential and subordinate. This was part of the school curriculum until 2007, when some of the rules were eliminated, but a shorter version was still included (Grace and Eng 2015). However, while cultural legacies remain powerful, a further key factor is surely that the political elite around Hun Sen has not wanted to make fundamental changes and has dominated the institutions of government, stifling political opposition and intimidating critical expression from journalists and NGOs (Marks and Naraharisetti 2013: 20).

Rwanda remains an authoritarian state with a poor record on human rights. Current economic policies exacerbate socioeconomic inequalities, leading to an increasing gap between women in remote rural areas and those occupying positions of political power (Cooper-Knock 2016). The increasingly autocratic leadership has also weakened autonomous women's movements, and, despite their increased participation, the ability of women to influence policy may have decreased (Burnet 2008: 363). Such points substantiate a more general argument that it is impossible to achieve gender justice without wider social justice, which ultimately also depends on civil and political freedoms creating space for autonomous campaigns, protests and political mobilisation. Yet the situation in Rwanda is far more advanced than that in Cambodia, as confirmed in the 2018 human development statistics, where the *Gender Inequality Index* ranks the two countries respectively at 85th (the highest in sub-Saharan Africa) and 116th. This contrasts with their general development rankings, where Rwanda is lower, at 158th, and Cambodia is 146th. Once again this demonstrates the specificity of each situation, as well as a high degree of indeterminacy: levels of development comprise only one of numerous factors that interact in complex ways.

Concluding Remarks

In a classic feminist text of the 1970s, Sheila Rowbotham demonstrated how women had been 'hidden from history' (Rowbotham 1973). By exposing and exploring the multiple sources of discrimination and oppression in the past, her purpose was also to contribute to a contemporary struggle for emancipation and equality. Similarly, as this chapter has shown, a combination of action on the ground and analysis has uncovered the ways in which victims and gender have been 'hidden from TJ'.

One task was to expose the inadequacies in the extent and nature of representation, particularly in the early stages of second-generation TJ. When present, victims were simply treated as witnesses in trials and TCs or as passive recipients of reparations. Women were largely 'absent' in defining TJ and in determining and implementing its mechanisms. Yet they were often particularly subject to abuses, and abuses of particular kinds, under repressive regimes and in civil wars, and they also played a key role in subsequently rebuilding societies.

As the chapter has shown, there has been limited progress in bringing about greater and more effective representation. Some courts have granted a role for victims in the prosecution process, and many TCs have provided support for those who testify. More outreach work has also been conducted in affected communities over the nature of reparations. Similarly, women have secured a stronger 'voice' in TJ, reflected in greater recognition of the fact that gender neutrality is often a mask for discrimination and inequality. There have also been legal developments on sexual and gender-based violence, more attention has been paid to the role of women in later TCs, and demands for gender-based reparations have grown. However, there are still profound and continuing shortcomings in conventional TJ.

One fundamental criticism in relation to victims has been that they tend to be viewed as 'objects' of TJ processes rather than as 'subjects' with their own agency, organisational ability and projects. There is often a gulf between the priorities of the most affected communities and those of national and international decision-makers, and sometimes there may even be a conceptual chasm between their different belief systems. At the same time conventional approaches tend to ignore the fact that the families of the disappeared have always played a key role in the development of TJ, extending its boundaries and showing that the search for truth and justice continues in the long-term.

Gender-based perspectives have provided still more penetrating critiques of conventional TJ. Benefiting from the 'second-wave feminism' of the 1960s and 1970s, theorists and practitioners have built on a body of existing scholarship to reveal the silences and omissions in mainstream approaches. There have, for example, been profound analyses of both the gendered aspects of law and the nature of justice and transition. Like victim-centred approaches, gendered perspectives have critiqued assumptions about passivity and have also uncovered some of the more subtle forms that this can take.

While the chapter has demonstrated the depth of the problems, it has not taken the view that victim and gender disadvantage are immutable and constant across all societies. Evidence about the position of women in four relatively poor and weak states thus suggests that progress towards greater gender equality, however limited, is not simply a function of the level of development or the type of political system. More generally, this again reinforces a more general conclusion that the impact of TJ is dependent upon the interaction of numerous forces, resulting in an important element of indeterminacy about outcomes.

One final point emerges from the chapter. Both perspectives provide many insights into TJ, raising issues that are often obscured in general evaluations or when the focus is solely on individual mechanisms. This would also be the case had the focus been on such overlapping themes as ethnicity, class and inequality or development. Yet there are some inevitable limitations in looking at TJ through any specific lens. For, however rich the contribution of an individual perspective may be, it cannot encompass all aspects of 'contending with the past'. I turn to this question in the final chapter.

5

Transitional Justice Today and Tomorrow

When TJ emerged as a field of theory and practice, it was marked by an intrinsic contradiction. It was a response to appalling human suffering, whether in repressive regimes or in episodes of mass violence or genocide, and in such circumstances it would be incongruous to describe it as an optimistic phenomenon. Yet its exponents certainly exuded confidence that it constituted part of a forward march to progress, informed by a commitment to liberal values. Underpinned by a belief in human rights and a determination to apply these in practice, TJ rested on an assumption that it was part of a new world order that would construct systems to banish the demons of the past. Some thirty years later, such confidence has eroded. Even the most ardent supporters of TJ recognise that the challenges are far greater than they had seemed, and the underlying international conditions that produced TJ have also changed markedly – largely in a negative direction. This chapter will consider some of the challenges and critiques, with the final section setting out my overall conclusions on the current situation and future prospects.

Debates and Critiques

Ever since its appearance as a recognisable and self-conscious field in the closing years of the twentieth century, TJ has developed in unforeseen ways, making it far more difficult to pin down conceptually and practically. While there were always sharp debates within the emerging field – for example, about judicial or non-judicial approaches and the relative importance of peace versus justice – there was also a degree of clarity about two central questions: how might there be accountability for past human rights atrocities in a transition from 'dictatorship', and would some forms of TJ be particularly conducive to the establishment of a stable liberal democracy? Of course the field had its critics from the early days, but the debates intensified as TJ became more complex and contested with its expansion into the world of peacebuilding. This had at least three effects.

Firstly, it accentuated the tendency to rely on a growing number of specialists who were keen to apply the lessons from one transition to another. Because peacebuilding was an international enterprise, centred in the major capitalist powers and often accompanied by intervention, there was a proliferation of international 'experts' and practitioners. TJ became one of the many tools through which the North and West attempted to reconstruct the ideas, institutions and systems of weaker states following violent conflict. Secondly, this global expansion brought the TJ community into countries and systems that were highly diverse and did not conform to the comparatively straightforward model trajectory that had underpinned the initial emergence of the field: many states in developing countries were not moving towards liberal democracy or even on the road to peace and stability. Thirdly, critical voices were amplified with the engagement with the Global South. The dominant framework of TJ remained liberal, but it was challenged with new critiques, partly as a result of confrontation with a wider range of theoretical perspectives and partly because of its difficulties in practice. Its adoption as an integral part of peacebuilding led it into situations of ongoing violence in a variety of different social, economic and political environments. The increasing scrutiny of weaknesses in implementation led to a de-centring of TJ both conceptually and practically. Some critical voices argue that it is currently entering a new generation, and there are profound debates about its legitimacy and effectiveness (Nesiah 2016: 5, 11). Padraig McAuliffe has also suggested that the more familiar approaches have now been displaced from the mainstream of TJ, at least in the specialist journals, while the more conventional mechanisms remain dominant in practice (McAuliffe 2017: 4). Without question, TJ is in a state of flux and uncertainty. What, then, are the main features of the current debates? These can be identified with reference to three closely related tensions within the subject: those between the international and the local, between 'top-down' and 'bottom-up' approaches, and between liberal and more radical ideas.

The West and Global North have played the leading role in defining, funding and implementing the mechanisms of TJ, while the majority of locations for putting them into practice have been in poorer states in the Global South. The ways in which this paradox is perceived constitute the first ongoing tension within the field. In general, the initial dominant perspective was to imply that the geopolitical location of the origins of the field was largely irrelevant. What was important was that TJ was developing new ideas about the importance of addressing the past and suggesting mechanisms for so doing. The task was to learn from experience so as to become more adept at tailoring practice to local realities. Furthermore, mainstream advocates of TJ insist that they are keen to facilitate and support voices and inputs from all the societies in which it is implemented. Acknowledging that there might have been too much emphasis in the early days on the idea of a 'model' or a 'toolbox' to be applied mechanistically, the more recent tendency has been to accept that TJ must be flexible and adapt to a variety of circumstances and situations and to claim that this is increasingly happening in practice. However, many critics do not accept this generally benign representation of the relationships, arguing that TJ was characterised by profound double standards from the start. The West may have promoted TJ as a means of addressing past atrocities, but it had supported many of the repressive regimes that carried out them out; and it favoured the idea of international jurisdiction to enforce universal norms against massive human rights abuses while ensuring that it was protected from such jurisdiction itself. Similarly, it continued to preside over a system of international political economy that had often contributed to the eruption of violence by undermining existing political systems in developing countries.

During the 1990s, the US and other leading Western powers were at least committed to promoting liberal values, albeit in partial ways, which were in harmony with the idea and practice of TJ. But 9/11 led to an immediate downgrading of international human rights promotion, with the 'war on terror' elevating the importance of security, and repressive regimes again received backing as allies. Inevitably, this led to a more problematic environment for TJ, as those activists who favoured radical transformative policies were now viewed as 'dangerous' in Washington. Clearly, more recent developments have intensified the pressures, leading to the shattering of the consensus that originally promoted the human rights norms. Rather than pressing for trials and TCs in former dictatorships, President Donald Trump praised a repressive leader, Rodrigo Duterte in the Philippines, who supported the summary killing of drug dealers rather than any form of judicial processes. In such circumstances, many are now deeply sceptical of claims that TJ has been a disinterested international development in the promotion of justice and argue instead for local initiatives and ownership of approaches to end impunity. The second key debate – about the relative importance of 'top-down' and 'bottom-up' approaches – relates closely to the international/local one.

The underlying assumption of conventional TJ, as it emerged in the latter years of the twentieth century, was that it was primarily a state-level process. States would effect transitions through national (or international or hybrid) trials, national TCs and reparation systems. Furthermore, the initial paradigm was that of a bargain between political elites, with the form of TJ agreed and implemented at national level, often located primarily in the capital city. Certainly, central mechanisms might be supplemented by more local involvement – for example, through outreach programmes or memorials – but these were not conceived as the primary way of bringing about change. However, as shown in earlier chapters, such approaches have frequently stimulated opposition or alienation among the mass of the population, particularly within the communities that suffered most from the repression or violence.

A limited form of 'bottom-up' approaches may be through unofficial 'truth projects', sometimes initiated when political leaders have refused to address the injustices of the past because of their own culpability or unwillingness to draw attention to potentially disruptive truths (Bickford 2007). These have included, for example, the Recovery of Historical Memory Project in Guatemala, which was ultimately highly influential in exposing the genocide there. Most projects of this kind were generated from 'below', though sometimes with very substantial involvement by lawyers and religious groups. The extent of leadership from above and below has varied, and in the commissions in Guatemala and Brazil the Church played a key role in 'fronting' and financing the work. But the Ardoyne Commemoration Project in Northern Ireland was launched entirely from the 'bottom up' in response to a 'whitewash' in an official investigation report (the Bloomfield Report of April 1998). This was an effort by members of a small Catholic working-class community, surrounded on three sides by Protestants, to remember the ninety-nine residents killed as a result of political violence (Lundy and McGovern 2008). 'Bottom-up' approaches can go much further than unofficial truth projects and may sometimes also seek to disrupt official approaches through sabotage and street protests, as, for example, in Nepal (Gready and Robins 2017: 963–70).

Some critical theorists within TJ have stressed the extent to which official approaches have derailed and undermined activists who were genuinely committed to overcoming impunity and transforming the underlying socioeconomic injustice that led to the initial repression and atrocities. Among a range of critics, Vesuki Nesiah demonstrates how the official approaches often attempt to bring about transitions through stressing consensus and common histories, thereby precluding the role of radical social movements, which played a key role in bringing about the downfall of the repressive regime. Such movements may press for a variety of differing agendas rather than those that promote a simplistic narrative to consolidate a transition (Nesiah 2016: 8–9, 42–8), and some critical analysts have explicitly argued that radical social movements from below need to achieve primacy in determining the future of TJ in theory and practice (Gready and Robins 2017). This leads to a third tension or debate: liberal versus radical perspectives on TJ.

Second-generation TJ was overwhelmingly associated with liberalism, and this was quite explicit in many of the early formulations. Subsequently, the liberalism often tended to become implicit rather than explicit, but the underlying assumptions remained broadly similar. However, following inputs into the debates from critical theory, development studies, gender studies, and various forms of radical and heterodox ideas, this consensus has now fragmented. There is perhaps no specifically Marxist or revolutionary theory of TJ, but, as McAuliffe has noted, there has been a 'transformative turn' in the subject, with the discourse of transformation proposing something more profound than stasis or reform (McAuliffe 2017: xiv). As noted in chapter 1, Rama Mani's pioneering critique of the dominant theory and practice of TJ and attempt to supplement it with the notion of 'reparative justice' was important in initiating this approach (Mani 2002, 2005). A further boost to this attempt to formulate alternative theories came in 2006 when the then UN High Commissioner on Human Rights, Louise Arbour, claimed that TJ was poised to 'make a significant leap', with the ambition of 'assisting the transformation of oppressed societies' through measures that 'would procure an equitable future'. This would involve also reaching beyond the 'crimes and abuses committed during the conflict' and addressing 'the human violations that pre-dated the conflict and caused, or contributed to it'. With such broad aims, TJ practitioners would probably 'expose a great number of discriminatory practices and violations of economic, social and cultural rights' (Arbour 2007: 2–3).

Such theories are diverse but tend to be united in criticising the original conventional approach for excluding key dimensions of injustice and, above all, socioeconomic and structural inequalities. Furthermore, the debates and tensions discussed above are also permeated by these differences of ideology and theory. Thus it is normally not just a question of whether the international or the local should have primacy or whether it is more effective to seek to bring about change from above or below, for these relationships are interpreted through different normative and theoretical frameworks. This may be elucidated by a consideration of three key concepts in TJ: transition, the nature of abuse, and justice.

The benchmark notion of a transition in the conventional approach to TJ has both a temporal and a normative aspect. It constitutes a transition *from* a situation of repression or violence *to* a new situation (that is, temporal change), but this representation of change is impregnated with the normative idea that stability and peace will be brought about through liberal democracy. From a more critical perspective, both the temporal and normative ideas in this schema can be challenged, for there may be no clear transition in either sense. The shift from dictatorship to a form of liberal democracy or from violence to 'peace' may mean a continuation of, rather than a break from, the pathologies that had been seen as abuses. For example, there may be continuity in high levels of violence or repression against indigenous peoples and women which had existed for generations. Against the conventional idea of 'transition', it might therefore be argued that this designation is itself a simplification of a complex situation, with the continuities as significant as the changes. Some critics go further and argue that this is not simply a misrepresentation of complexity but a way of framing the situation in terms of transition so as to close down some forms of challenge to the new or continuing status quo (Nesiah 2016: 48). For example, it may be in the interests of elite forces in a society to suggest that there has been a major transformation (from dictatorship to democracy or from war to peace) so as to legitimise their power and de-legitimise those who challenge it. The designation of a situation as one of transition, partially through TJ, and acceptance of this description could help to consolidate elite interests in constructing a liberal regime.

This leads to a second conceptual critique, which questions the nature of the abuses that are to be remedied. The main focus of TJ mainstream theory and practice has been to address past overt violence and forms of dictatorial repression. But this again has led to critiques about definition and causation. As many have argued, physical violence is normally a manifestation of deeper forms of structural and cultural violence, which may continue even when there is a reduction in the visible manifestations addressed by TJ – at least in the short term. Thus it has been argued that TJ should focus on the elimination of these structural causes. Similarly, it should view repression, atrocities and violence in a more profound sense by addressing them in relation to class, history, gender relations, racism and the economy. Otherwise such approaches as trials, TCs and reparations will be superficial and ineffective, or even diversions through which the *claim* of addressing past crimes enables the structures and social sectors primarily responsible for them to continue.

Finally, a third critique is levelled at the conception of justice itself in the conventional view. This has been

charged with being too backward looking, too individual-
istic, too concerned with the judicial criminal sphere, and
too focused on bringing about accountability for overt
physical violations. As foreshadowed in chapter 1 and
demonstrated throughout the book, such critiques have led
to an accumulation of concepts of justice, including socioeconomic justice, historical justice, gender justice, global
justice and transformative justice. And, in some versions, the
critique includes specifying the necessary path to bring about
such goals, often incorporating a position in relation to the
tensions discussed above.

Paul Gready and Simon Robins have thus argued that
transformative change is a 'change that emphasizes local
agency and resources, the prioritization of process rather
than preconceived outcomes and the challenging of unequal
and intersecting power relationships and structures of
exclusion at both the local and the global level' (Gready
and Robins 2014: 340). Transformative justice, they argue,
seeks not to dismiss or replace TJ but radically to reform its
politics, locus and priorities. More recently they have refined
the theory, focusing on the idea of 'justice in transition',
suggesting that this is a conceptual term or framework,
while transformative justice is a form of practice or activism,
designed as a means of delivering justice in transition. The
key agency, to which they ascribe a pivotal role in bringing
about the transformative change, is assigned to what they
term 'new civil society', associated with such events as the
Arab Spring and austerity-led protests in Southern Europe.
While mainstream TJ views NGOs as constituting civil
society, which privileges advocacy, support and capacity-
building, with the state and state institutions as the main
points of reference, new civil society champions autonomy,
independent action and the modelling of alternatives, often
choosing not to see the state as a principal reference (Gready
and Robins 2017: 957–8). Their core arguments are that
rethinking civil society entails rethinking modes of organisation, repertories of action, and understandings of politics,
rights and justice, as well as of transnational approaches. All

this entails a broader discussion of justice, with both conceptualisation and activism needing to 'evolve southward',
placing TJ 'closer to the pulse of contemporary activism and
protest' (ibid.: 970).

All these debates call into question the boundaries of TJ
and the relationship between the theory and practice of the
field in the 1990s and the situation now. Does TJ have an
ineradicable core, or is it subject to a continual process of
transmutation as a result of constant critique? I will return
to this issue in the final section, but first it is necessary to
consider some further contemporary challenges.

New Challenges

Because TJ is constantly evolving, it continually faces new
challenges, often from long-standing issues that have only
recently become formulated as specific concerns. One example
is that of corporate responsibility for human rights abuses.
This was belatedly considered by the South African Truth and
Reconciliation Commission, but in an unsatisfactory way,
leading to the campaign against 'economic apartheid' by the
Khulumani organisation discussed in the previous chapter.
Subsequently, the issue of corporate responsibility has been
highlighted in several countries. In 2014–15, Argentina took
significant steps, including corporate complicity trials, the
establishment of a unit within the Ministry of Justice to
examine the issue, and a decision by the parliament to create
a special investigatory commission. The question is also of
central importance in Colombia, where corporate interests
were deeply implicated in state and paramilitary violence
throughout the civil war. The peace settlement initially
envisaged provisions for robust action to be taken, but the
prospects for implementation appeared to diminish with the
election of the right-wing president in 2018. If so, this would
follow the pattern set in several other countries, where
corporate responsibility for violations has been highlighted
but only partially followed up. The topic is clearly extremely
important, but, as with other aspects of entrenched power,

effective responses have tended to elude TJ and no doubt demand more fundamental transformations, politically and economically.

A further challenge is to overcome the dominance of European languages, above all English, in TJ. This effectively discriminates against those using other languages in discussions about theory and practice and, of still greater concern, means that even genuine attempts to work with indigenous peoples may be impeded. For example, a national reparations programme in Guatemala encountered real problems when attempting to translate 'reparation' into Q'eqchi' because the concept does not exist in this language. Such problems are, of course, only one aspect of the more general phenomenon of Western and Northern domination, but they highlight an additional dimension of the tendency of TJ to be remote from peoples that it seeks to reach. Any serious attempt to tackle this depends upon reversing such linguistic hegemony.

There are many such challenges, and this brief section examines three of them in a little more depth.

(a) The cultural sphere

A comparatively recent development has been to emphasise the importance of cultural and artistic developments within the canon of TJ. To some extent this has long been acknowledged – for example, in relation to memorialisation – but a current trend is to regard the cultural sphere as an integral rather than a peripheral dimension. This coming of age received a seal of approval with an edited book of almost 600 pages, backed by the International Center of Transitional Justice (Ramírez-Barat 2014; see also Rush and Simić 2014; Newman 2016). This takes the topic in a broad sense and includes contributions on outreach work and the media and justice, as well as discussions of participatory theatre, testimony, photography, memorialisation and literature. In his introductory essay, Pablo de Greiff suggests that cultural products and activities can surpass some of the more formal instruments of TJ, for they can raise awareness of the depth, breadth and effects of rights violations; be 'more effective at representing pain, suffering, indignation, and rage, as well as determination, endurance, and dignity'; be more adept at capturing the complexity of the social and intergenerational effects; and provide means of expression for victims and survivors that are not open to them through the formal discourse of citizenship (de Greiff 2014: 18–20). These are important points, but care is needed when considering the relationship between TJ and culture.

In some cases, the connections seem obvious. Several commentators have noted an early example of this in Ariel Dorfman's play *Death and the Maiden*, which emerged from, and vividly represented the dilemmas of, the transition from the Pinochet dictatorship to a constrained form of democracy in Chile (McAuliffe 2014; Newman 2016). It is also notable that one of the most trenchant and insightful critical theorists of TJ, Rama Mani, has now turned to art forms, including poetry, to convey some of the themes arising from injustice and conflict (Mani and Kelly 2017). Similarly, through numerous genres, communities have always turned to art forms as vehicles for the expression and communication of issues of justice and injustice, sometimes also linking these to questions about transitions. The Kenyan writer Ngũgĩ wa Thiong'o, for example, used community theatre to expose the continuities between colonial and post-colonial rule and the fact that there had been little substantive transformation (Newman 2016: 87–117). More generally, fiction may illuminate the complexity of the concepts of injustice, justice and transition, providing a different perspective from that of the social sciences. This is specifically because it depicts and encapsulates collective situations through the subjective sphere, lived experiences and creative imagination (ibid.: 213–26). People certainly contend with the past through culture, and analysis of this sphere contributes to a multidimensional understanding of TJ.

Yet there are dangers in attempting to harness culture to any official and institutional mechanisms, for this may shackle it to a particular agenda. As Catherine Cole has noted, artists often value 'opacity, ambiguity, irony, indirection, instability, indeterminacy of meaning, deep questioning of norms and disruption of linear narratives' (Cole 2014: 315). The proposal of a marriage between TJ and the cultural sphere thus raises crucial questions about TJ itself. Certainly, cultural interventions often highlight questions that tend to be understated in conventional approaches. For example, they reveal the ways in which perceptions of justice and injustice are fluid and changeable so that the idea of 'fixing a problem' by a particular mechanism or at a specific time is inappropriate. Similarly, the ways in which structural and historical injustice permeate relationships may be profoundly embedded in consciousness and revealed more fully through the arts than in the realms of politics and legality. That the realm of culture can offer much to the understanding of justice and injustice thus seems demonstrable. The question is rather whether TJ is sufficiently open to different voices to accept insights derived from the arts. If TJ is itself 'instrumentalist', it will not do so, but if it is more malleable and shaped by pressures from below, the contribution of culture becomes more important. In this way the cultural sphere can certainly add a dimension to TJ by demonstrating the multiple layers of justice, injustice and transition, and it would be helpful for domestic and international authorities to facilitate artistic endeavours. But this is quite different from suggesting that TJ should seek to use or control the arts to promote a particular narrative, the dangers of which have often been revealed in relation to memorialisation.

(b) Climate change and the environment

If, as is widely agreed, climate change, with its consequential irreparable planetary damage, is the most dangerous current threat to the world, it would seem inappropriate for the topic to be ignored in debates about TJ. Furthermore, its relevance becomes still more evident when the relationships between climate change and issues of war, peace and human rights are considered. Identification of a precise causal relationship between environmental degradation and violent conflict is contentious, but desertification has certainly been a factor in contributing to such violence, including in Rwanda, Sudan (Darfur), Mali and Syria (Leroy 2009; Grene and Cammaer 2017). This does not, of course, substantiate a reductionist claim that climate change has *caused* the human rights violations, but certainly the social and climatic factors are very often combined. There is also overwhelming evidence that environmental catastrophes tend to occur in the poorest countries, and normally the most vulnerable communities, such as indigenous peoples in remote areas, are the worst affected. This was, for example, reflected in the attempts of the Inuit of Northern Alaska and Canada to secure action by the Inter-American Commission on Human Rights on their complaint that global warming, caused by gases from the US, violated their right to sustain their traditional modes of life (Burkett 2009: 519–20). Furthermore, in 2009, Navanethem Pillay, the then UN High Commissioner for Human Rights, presented a report on the relationship between climate change and human rights which specified the observed and projected changes in weather patterns that would potentially have implications for the full range of human rights. Under the most basic 'right to life', this noted that the rights to adequate food, water, health, housing and self-determination could not be fully exercised due to climate disasters (UN 2009: paras. 21–4).

There are thus strong interrelationships between climate change, environmental degradation and human rights violations, and it has been suggested that this sphere should be included within TJ. In March 2013, Joy Hyvarinen, the then executive director of the Foundation for International Environmental Law and Development, presented a paper on 'Climate Change and Global Justice: Lessons from Transitional Justice?' at an international economics congress in Berlin. This argued that a TJ approach, for example through truth processes, might be required so as to tackle the climate change necessary for global justice, while also making reconciliation and co-operation possible (quoted in Szablewska and Bachmann 2015: 356). Here, and in a paper again drawn from TJ theories, Hyvarinen argued that reparations for the victims of climate change would be an important possible development to bring about global justice (Hyvarinen 2015). Maxine Burkett also drew on the work of Martha Minow and, still more fully, Pablo de Greiff on reparations in the context of TJ in her own attempt to develop an overarching reparations claim necessitated by climate change (Burkett 2009: 521–3, 531–5). The argument that TJ, suitably adapted, could help to secure a more satisfactory international response to the problems has thus led to some debate within the climate change community, but the key question here is whether its inclusion would be beneficial for TJ.

There has been some support for the idea. For example, Alessandro Pelizzon has put forward a theoretical and conceptual argument suggesting that all human societies are now in an era of ongoing environmental transition, which makes it appropriate to rethink our concepts of conflict, bringing back the idea of humans 'at war with nature'. He also holds that the notion of justice needs to be extended beyond an anthropocentric view towards an ecocentric one (Pelizzon 2015). More concretely, Szablewska and Bachmann argue that TJ might need to undergo its greatest paradigm shift thus far with environmental issues and climate change. Emphasising the existing relationships between environmental degradation and conflict, including the centrality of water and the still greater impact of climate change in the future, they insist that this entails an extended understanding of transition 'from the world as we know it to the new and not yet fully imagined future of massive degradation of ecosystems beyond the point of repair' (Szablewska and Bachmann 2015: 358). They conclude that, for TJ, an agenda for the future might be not *if*, but *how* the natural environment and its relationship to humans 'affects the prospects for maintaining and rebuilding viable and long-term peace and stability' (ibid.: 359).

As yet, this is a minority view within TJ, but these issues will obviously not go away, and the relationships between the environment and the central concerns of TJ are sometimes brought into sharp relief. For example, Global Witness has reported that 200 environmental activists, wildlife rangers and indigenous leaders trying to protect their land were killed in 2016, more than double the numbers killed five years ago, and the rate increased during 2017. John Knox, the UN Special Rapporteur on Human Rights and the Environment, has also highlighted the culture of impunity that has been developing. This has led to a growing sense that environmental defenders could be killed without repercussions, while the people most at risk are those who are already marginalised and dependent on the environment (Watts and Vidal 2017). These are not the 'mass atrocities' that have been the central concern of TJ, and nor are they necessarily in situations of obvious transition, but they highlight some of the issues emphasised by those who call for marriage between TJ and the forms of global justice sought by climate change and environmental campaigners.

(c) Transitional justice in established liberal democracies

A further challenge again concerns the temporal understanding of 'transition'. As already discussed, the conventional paradigm holds that TJ is introduced in circumstances where there is an obvious transition – classically that of a change of regime or after a violent conflict. In fact, this textbook timetable for implementation has not always been followed even in conventional usages. International criminal law in relation to mass atrocities often developed in situations of ongoing violent conflict – for example, the International Criminal Tribunal for the former Yugoslavia was established during the war itself rather than at its end. Yet this tribunal and both its counterpart in Rwanda and the ICC itself are conventionally seen as important mechanisms of TJ. More recently, there have been attempts to implement other forms of TJ in ongoing conflicts, as for example with initiatives in Colombia long before the signing of the peace, which may have been helpful steps towards the settlement (García-Godos 2012; van Nievelt 2016). Such discussions challenge the conventional notion that TJ *follows* a transition. Arguments that TJ also has relevance to long-established stable regimes raise still more acute challenges.

The relevance of TJ in this context has been suggested with particular reference to such settler colonies as Australia, New Zealand, Canada and the US in relation to the treatment of indigenous communities. The fact that the construction of these states was carried out by the violent suppression of the existing populations, and the elimination of their customs, practices and rights to land, is well documented, and movements for justice have long existed in relation to these wrongs. But it is a recent development to mount such campaigns in the name of TJ. One point that unites those who argue in favour of its relevance is dissatisfaction with other ways of conceptualising and implementing redress for these forms of injustice. Most commonly, these have suggested that there has been a 'historical injustice', but the underlying assumption of such positions has normally been that these former settler colonies subsequently evolved into stable liberal-democracies and that the idea of transition (and therefore also TJ) is therefore inappropriate. Advocacy of its relevance undermines such complacency by insisting that a transition is still necessary, since the injustices at the time of the foundation and construction of the original settler state continue to negate the professed claims of the current liberal order. There therefore needs to be a 'transition from unjust relations to just relations', and this suggests the relevance of TJ (Balint et al. 2014: 214).

There are also differences among the proponents of this view. Steven Winter grounds his case in liberal political theory, suggesting that the settler states did not possess legitimacy when they operated on the basis of a racism that 'justified the degradation and dispossession of the indigenous peoples by deeming them inferior' (Winter 2014: 73–5).

The establishment of legitimacy has required a continuing process of redress, but, in Winter's view, the transition has now taken place, as the states have acknowledged and tried to overcome their past wrongdoing. Others take a more radical view, arguing that the original forms of injustice remain embedded in current practices, institutional racism and cultural attitudes (Hobbs 2016; Balint et al. 2014). Such analyses thus draw attention to long-term structural aspects of societies that account for the continuing differential life chances of settler and indigenous communities. From this perspective, TJ, through a restoration of liberal legitimacy, is quite insufficient: what is needed is a structural transformation that seeks to overcome the cumulative injustices that have been perpetuated through history and are constantly reinforced. The debates between liberal and more radical approaches to TJ thus continue when the temporal boundaries of the subject are extended.

Conclusion

As this chapter has shown, there are now several related debates within TJ which challenge conventional understandings of the field. They raise the question of whether it has an ineradicable core or whether it is characterised by a continual process of transmutation. On the one hand, it might be suggested that an inclusive and open-ended attitude towards theory and practice demonstrates a willingness to learn from other areas and to allow TJ practices to be implemented in any ways that seem appropriate in a wide variety of circumstances. On the other hand, as Christine Bell has suggested, the capacity of TJ constantly to expand in reach, with increasing ambiguities, makes it resemble a miracle fabric 'whose warp and weave contain an almost infinite stretchiness' (Bell 2016: 3). The question of whether this malleability is problematic or beneficial surely depends on whether TJ contains a sufficiently robust core in theoretical, normative and practical terms both to benefit from these enlargements of focus and to contribute to the resolution of crucial problems in relation to both transitions and justice.

It is hardly surprising that some proponents of TJ have opposed both the proposed enlargement of focus and key aspects of the critical approaches. Such concerns often centre on the dangers that the extension of ambition will render it ineffective. Lars Waldorf, for example, has argued that both overloading and underfunding create practical problems in any attempts by TCs or reparations to address socioeconomic wrongs, and that remedying injustices of this kind is a long-term project, while TJ mechanisms have relatively short lifespans. More generally, he concludes that well-meaning efforts to address socioeconomic inequalities through TJ will simply burden it with yet more unrealisable expectations (Waldorf 2012: 179–81). Similarly, Padraig McAuliffe has provided a detailed critique of 'the transformative turn' (McAuliffe 2017). His fundamental argument, based on both analytical theory and empirical evidence, is that transformative scholarship has failed to address key questions about the distribution of power and barriers to change, particularly in complex and difficult post-conflict environments. Proponents of such approaches, he suggests, show a propensity to see the world as infinitely malleable and to presume that the immediate period of transition provides an opportunity for substantial changes in both institutions and the political order. Concentrating on three key variables – the functionality of the state, the nature of domestic politics and the economic situation – McAuliffe argues that, particularly in poor and weak states at the bottom of the development ladder, the potential for transformation in a post-conflict transition is very limited and that, in the absence of a unified domestic will, external actors can bring about little change in socioeconomic structures (ibid.: 29, 295 and chapter 4). Exaggerating the possibilities of transformation, he suggests, represents a mix of narcissism and hand-wringing when everything that is known about post-conflict states suggests that TJ has 'neither the potential ascribed to it to change structures of injustice nor the complicity in them it damns itself with' (ibid.: 297). It is, he concludes, important neither to exaggerate nor deprecate its effects as a force for political and social change.

Such critics often emphasise questions of practicality, arguing that attempting or promising too much will lead to overextension and failure, which will have a negative impact both on the areas in which TJ is implemented and on the credibility of the field. Yet theoretical and normative assumptions about the conceptual core of TJ lie beneath these practical questions. The implicit supposition is that the central concerns should be defined by the essentially liberal doctrines that dominated the field as it emerged in the 1980s and 1990s. Extensive departure from this framework will, it is assumed, be problematic. However, many of the critics of the more conventional approaches are equally convinced of the contrary view: that a field that was once innovative and dynamic 'now travels as a stable repertoire of normative assumptions, institutional forms and policy prescriptions' and seeks acceptance within the mainstream of post-conflict policy rather than to push for social change (Nesiah 2016: 11). This perspective holds that TJ needs to recover its original mission: to seek an end to impunity and to exploit the transformative opportunities of transitions for radical change. At root, then, the debate is about the 'essence' of TJ and what constitutes its importance. Can this dispute be resolved?

The architects of TJ as a self-conscious theory and practice were driven by a desire to create a better world where neither atrocities and mass human rights violations nor revenge killings and executions would be acceptable. They were seeking to promote effective means of responding to the past by peaceful forms of redress, but they also regarded it as unacceptable to follow the Spanish example, in which the transition from Franco's dictatorship was established on the basis of amnesia about the brutal repression that had been carried out during and after the civil war. A fundamentally liberal conception of politics and rights quickly became dominant in the definition, elaboration and implementation of TJ, but this had not been the case in the wider social movements that had called for accountability and justice in Latin America in the 1980s and 1990s. Nor, I would suggest, is TJ inevitably embedded in liberalism, for it is compatible with far more radical positions.

The central concerns of TJ surely remain crucially important. Certainly, there have been differing opinions as to whether it is always beneficial to address the horrors of the past and whether a need to do so is shared across all societies. At one extreme, Kathryn Sikkink implies near universality, asserting that TJ has been taken up across the world partly because some ideas catch on when 'related to deeper ideational instincts in the human brain'. The ideas of justice and the punishment of those who violate social norms, she suggests, are deeply embedded in many societies around the world, meaning that there is an initial receptivity to demands for justice because humans intrinsically find certain human rights appealing (Sikkink 2011: 261). This no doubt goes beyond the evidence, and many have suggested that different cultures have quite distinct ways of addressing the past which do not conform to this approach. For several years Mozambique was seen as an example of a country that had moved on without needing to dwell on its past. Recently, though, this was called into question when there was a claim that the passing of an amnesty law and avoidance of any form of TJ simply served the interests of the victors of the civil war and did not imply any cultural predisposition to forget (Igreja 2015).

Hard evidence about the extent to which TJ responds to universal needs no doubt lies buried beneath layers of complex interrelationships between the nature of human beings and social, political, economic and cultural dimensions of behaviour. Yet there is also good reason for scepticism about some claims that TJ is simply a Western imposition. As Chandra Lekha Sriram has noted in a generally critical discussion of TJ within liberal peace-building, external actors often face demands from indigenous governments and NGOs for accountability for past atrocities

(Sriram 2007: 591). And many suggestions that particular countries have disregarded abuses of the past simply because of specific cultural norms are barely credible. For example, in China, episodes such as 'the Great Leap Forward', the Cultural Revolution, and the massacres of Tiananmen Square are taboo, and Japan has also failed to scrutinise its own past. Such refusals surely emanate primarily from state policies rather than from cultural norms, and the distorted versions of history that they produce continue to have damaging internal effects and inflame relations between the two countries (McGregor 2017). Similarly, Israel's refusal to address its responsibility for the Nakba,[1] while constantly defining itself in terms of the Holocaust, has very negative consequences, as have the currently revisionist approaches to history in Hungary, Poland, Russia and Turkey. This failure adequately to address their own histories, or to do so in damaging self-justificatory ways, also applies to most of the leading Western powers, which have been keen to impose TJ on weaker states in the South while refusing to consider it at home. However, in contrast to David Rieff's claim, quoted in chapter 2, that there are cases where there is a 'duty to forget' (Rieff 2016: 121), I would argue that the most fundamental justification of TJ should be through an insistence that the past must be addressed in an open, critical way rather than in a partisan myth-making one.

Of course, in practice TJ often fails to meet this criterion, for new regimes use the opportunity to produce convenient narratives of their own rather than contending with the complexities of the past. But, at their best, TCs and forms of memorialisation have been very valuable in this respect. The timing and manner of this confrontation with history may be infinitely variable, but seeking to address the past is the core concern of TJ and the foundation for its importance in other respects. This does not make it inevitable that it will take place everywhere, and populations that have been most

---

[1] That is, 'the disaster', referring to the expulsion and flight of approximately 700,000 Palestinians during the 1948 war.

affected by violence and repression may often be more preoccupied with remedies for socioeconomic deprivation. In such circumstances, TJ should certainly not be imposed, for it needs to develop organically. Nevertheless, Christine Bell is surely right in suggesting that failing to provide constructive spaces for contending with the past will not resolve the problem but divert contention to other arenas, which may not be peaceful and may undermine the legitimacy of a post-conflict state (Bell 2016: 20). To take just one example, it seems likely that a partial explanation of the extreme bitterness in the relationship between the government in Madrid and the Catalonian independence movement may be partly attributable to the failure to contend with the past in the aftermath of the Franco dictatorship.[2]

If, then, TJ has a central focus of concern and a continuing importance, what conclusions may be drawn about the tensions and debates discussed earlier in this chapter? The first is that such contestation should be regarded as inherent in the subject and potentially beneficial. Critics have been justified in emphasising the international domination over TJ processes and the fact that powerful states have often used these for their own purposes with little regard for local preferences. Similarly, national elites have tended to control domestic procedures in TJ, often with minimal consideration for 'bottom-up' initiatives or the position of marginal or vulnerable communities. Governments in weaker states have also sometimes manipulated international mechanisms or have exploited the discourse of TJ as a mask to protect their own impunity. For all these reasons, local-level and 'bottom-up' projects can obviously be highly beneficial, both to participants and to a wider community.

Yet it also seems unlikely that social movements can implement alternative forms of TJ on any but a local scale without some national, and often international, involvement. Viewed historically, TJ has developed through processes of both contradiction and fusion between these different

---

[2] I am grateful to Sebastian Balfour for suggesting this point.

elements, and it is therefore unhelpful to pose the relationships in dichotomous terms. For example, there has been a reciprocal interaction in the evolution of TCs: some unofficial ones pre-date official initiatives, which then drew on them – as for example in Guatemala – or official TCs, generating other forms of truth-telling, sometimes in opposition to them – as in Sierra Leone. Even when the relationship between official forms of TJ and civil society appears the most antagonistic, mutual interdependence remains. In Nepal, for example, the systems of TJ to which the political elites have paid lip service may be wholly removed from the priorities and needs of victims. But it is perhaps unlikely that a network and movement to challenge the current policies of the Nepalese government and to seek to bring about an alternative approach would have developed without some input based on international experiences in TJ.

A second and related conclusion is that diverse theoretical and normative conceptions, leading to differing policy implications, are also bound to coexist within TJ. Many practitioners, well versed in international expertise, may emphasise the familiar mechanisms, albeit with greater flexibility than in the past, while critical theorists will continue to argue that conventional TJ views the key problems too narrowly. They will, for example, insist that gender injustice inheres in cultural and structural spheres that lie beyond the realms of civil and political rights, and that mass violations are normally embedded in structural and historical injustices and cannot ultimately be eradicated without addressing the deep inequalities that normally remain intact long after TJ measures have been implemented. Similarly, radical critics will justifiably argue that effective policies will require pressure from below through mobilisation of civil society movements. Ultimately, as proponents of global justice insist, action will also be needed to address the international structures that do so much to generate overt violence and atrocities. At the same time, others will criticise such ideas on the grounds that they are impracticable and overestimate the potential for transformative TJ. Yet, despite the apparent paradox, I would suggest that there are important truths in both positions and that it is unnecessary to endorse either of them to the exclusion of the other.

It may be entirely valid to argue that in many situations the extent of conceivable change is extremely restricted, and that those who talk of fundamental socioeconomic trans-formation are being quite unrealistic. But it does not follow that the theoretical conceptions underpinning TJ need to be equally limited. Informed analysis may reveal very limited possibilities in a given situation, but critical insights may still demonstrate that conventional TJ will do little to remedy the underlying problems in the long-term. An acceptance of 'reality' is not a good reason to abandon more extensive notions of what is ultimately necessary; and critiques under-pinning fuller conceptions of justice may reveal further pressures and openings that may not be apparent if it is always assumed in advance that a very restricted form of TJ is all that is possible. As Bronwyn Anne Leebaw noted, the struggle against state-sponsored atrocities requires the ongoing critical work of activists and scholars engaged in challenging political realities 'with new efforts to imagine and demand a world that is more just' (Leebaw 2012: 306). All this would suggest that it is both possible and advan-tageous to regard TJ as a field that necessarily contains tensions and internal debates. How does this relate to the boundaries of the field?

In my view, the defining parameters for TJ are that it is concerned with contending with the past in ways that are compatible with the origins of the field – a search for justice, combined with a commitment to human rights and a rejection of violence, including the violence of capital punishment and revenge killings. These parameters do not specify the definition of justice or human rights – whether confined to the civil, political and judicial spheres or extending far wider, as in more transformative versions. Nor do they seek to define the nature of violence – whether it is restricted to overt bodily violence or is seen to lie in more subtle cultural and structural terms. Nor, finally, does it provide a specific interpretation of a 'transition', although I would suggest that something approaching the original notion, rather than in wider conceptions such as that of established states or in relation to climate change, will remain the norm.

How, then, should TJ be viewed in the world of today and tomorrow? As suggested at the beginning of this chapter, its birth was contradictory – marked by its simultaneous association with atrocities and an optimistic belief that a new form of justice could overcome them – and contradictions continue to be hard-wired into its DNA. For, even in the most favourable circumstances, the path for societies emerging from repression or violent conflict is likely to be bumpy, making it unrealistic to expect too much from TJ, which is simply one element within a transition. It is therefore surely also inevitable that those who seek to evaluate it will be divided between those who view the glass as half empty and those who see it as half full. Yet it has made crucial advances in understanding ways to contend with the past and has had important elements of success. Through the management of its internal tensions and debates, it can continue as one element within a wider movement that helps to build a better future. In its origins, it included both liberal and more radical forces, which were able to unite in favour of contending with the past and seeking to ensure that impunity would be eradicated. The current need is to rebuild this kind of coalition so as to facilitate an eventual change in the international power structures and normative climate. In this way TJ could re-emerge as a movement for human rights in its most expansive form without being tainted by the current economic framework and system of international power that has so limited its potential.

References

Abdullah, H. (2014) Women organising for gender equality in Sierra Leonean politics, *Democracy in Africa*, http://democracyinafrica. org/women-organising-gender-equality-sierra-leonean-politics/.

Ainley, K. (2017) Evaluating the evaluators: transitional justice and the contest of values, *International Journal of Transitional Justice*, 11(3): 421–42.

Ainley, K., Friedman, R., and Mahony, C. (2015) The potential and politics of transitional justice: interactions between the global and the local in evaluations of success, in Ainley, K., Friedman, R., and Mahony, C. (eds), *Evaluating Transitional Justice: Accountability and Peacebuilding in Post-Conflict Sierra Leone*. Basingstoke: Palgrave Macmillan.

Allen, T., and Macdonald, A. (2013) *Post-Conflict Traditional Justice: A Critical Overview*, LSE JSRP Paper 3, http://eprints. lse.ac.uk/56357/1/JSRP_Paper3_Post-conflict_traditional_ justice_Allen_Macdonald_2013.pdf.

Arbour, L. (2007) Economic and social justice for societies in transition, *New York University Journal of International Law and Politics*, 40(1): 1–27.

Arnould, V., and Sriram, C. L. (2014) *Pathways of Impact: How Transitional Justice Affects Democratic Institution-Building*, TJDI Policy Paper 1, www.egmontinstitute.be/content/ uploads/2014/10/TJDI-Policy-Paper-Pathways-of-Impact1. pdf?type=pdf.

Arriaza, L., and Roht-Arriaza, N. (2008) Social reconstruction as a local process, *International Journal of Transitional Justice*, 2(2): 152–72.

Arthur, P. (2009) How 'transitions' reshaped human rights: a conceptual history of transitional justice, *Human Rights Quarterly*, 31(2): 321–67.

Asian Development Bank (2014) *Timor-Leste Country Gender Assessment*, www.adb.org/sites/default/files/institutional-document/84126/timor-leste-country-gender-assessment.pdf.

Bakiner, O. (2014) Truth commission impact: an assessment of how commissions influence politics and society, *International Journal of Transitional Justice*, 8(1): 6–30.

Bakiner, O. (2016) *Truth Commissions: Memory, Power, and Legitimacy*. Philadelphia: University of Pennsylvania Press.

Balint, J., Evans, J., and McMillan, N. (2014) Rethinking transitional justice, redressing indigenous harm: a new conceptual approach, *International Journal of Transitional Justice*, 8(2): 194–216.

Bates, G., Cinar, I., and Nalepa, M. (2017) *Purges and Truth Revelation Procedures 1946–2016: Introducing a Transitional Justice Dataset*, University of Chicago Working Paper, www.monikanalepa.com/uploads/6/6/3/1/66318923/2111_personneltjdataset_.pdf.

Bell, C. (2009) Transitional justice, interdisciplinarity and the state of the 'field' or 'non-field', *International Journal of Transitional Justice*, 3(1): 5–27.

Bell, C. (2016) *The Fabric of Transitional Justice*, University of Edinburgh, School of Law, Research Paper no. 2016/22.

Bell, C. (2017) The fabric of transitional justice: binding local and global political settlements, in Bell, C. (ed.), *Transitional Justice*. Abingdon: Routledge.

Bell, C., and O'Rourke, C. (2007) Does feminism need a theory of transitional justice? An introductory essay, *International Journal of Transitional Justice*, 1(1): 23–44.

Bell, C., Campbell, C., and Ní Aoláin, F. (2007) The battle for transitional justice: hegemony, Iraq, and international law, in Morison, J., McEvoy, K., and Anthony, G. (eds), *Judges, Transition, and Human Rights*. Oxford: Oxford University Press.

Bickford, L. (2007) Unofficial truth projects, *Human Rights Quarterly*, 29(4): 994–1035.

Bickford, L. (2014) Memoryworks/Memory works, in

Ramírez-Barat, C. (ed.), *Transitional Justice, Culture, and Society: Beyond Outreach*. New York: Social Science Research Council, Columbia University Press.

Borger, J. (2017) Bosnians divided over Ratko Mladić guilty verdict for war crimes, *The Guardian*, 22 November, www.theguardian.com/world/2017/nov/22/bosnians-divided-over-ratko-mladic-guilty-verdict-for-war-crimes.

Bosco, D. (2014) *Rough Justice: The International Criminal Court in a World of Power Politics*. Oxford: Oxford University Press.

Brahm, E. (2007) Uncovering the truth: examining truth commission success and impact, *International Studies Perspectives*, 8(1): 16–35.

Branch, D. (2011) *Kenya between Hope and Despair, 1963–2011*. New Have, CT: Yale University Press.

Brounéus, K. (2010) Truth-telling as talking cure? Insecurity and retraumatization in the Rwandan gacaca courts, *Security and Dialogue*, 39(1): 55–76.

Buckley-Zistel, S., and Zolkos, M. (2012) Introduction: gender in transitional justice, in Buckley-Zistel, S., and Stanley, R. (eds). *Gender in Transitional Justice*. Basingstoke: Palgrave Macmillan.

Buckley-Zistel, S., Koloma Beck, T., Braun, C., and Mieth, F. (eds) (2014) *Transitional Justice Theories*. Abingdon: Routledge.

Burkett, M. (2009) Climate reparations, *Melbourne Journal of International Law*, 10(2): 509–42.

Burnet, J. E. (2008) Gender balance and the meanings of women in governance in post-genocide Rwanda, *African Affairs*, 107(428): 361–86.

Burnet, J. E. (2012) *Genocide Lives in Us: Women, Memory, and Silence in Rwanda*. Madison: University of Wisconsin Press.

CAMBOW (Cambodian Committee of Women) (2007) *Violence against Women: How Cambodian Laws Discriminate against Women*, www.licadho-cambodia.org/reports/files/112CAMBOWViolenceWomenReport2007_ENG.pdf.

Carranza, R., Correa, C., and Naughton, E. (2015) *More Than Words: Apologies as a Form of Reparation*. New York: International Center for Transitional Justice, www.ictj.org/sites/default/files/ICTJ-Report-Apologies-2015.pdf.

Castillejo, C. (2009) *Women's Political Participation and Influence in Sierra Leone*, FRIDE Working Paper no. 83, http://fride.org/descarga/wp83_women_political_eng_jun09.pdf.

CEH (Commission for Historical Clarification) (1999) *Guatemala: Memory of Silence, Report of the Commission for Historical Clarification: Conclusions and Recommendations*, https://hrdag.org/wp-content/uploads/2013/01/CEHreport-english.pdf.

Chapman, A. (2008) Perspectives on the role of forgiveness in the human rights violations hearings, in Chapman, A., and van der Merwe, H. (eds), *Truth and Reconciliation in South Africa: Did the TRC Deliver?* Philadelphia: University of Pennsylvania Press.

Chapman, A., and Ball, P. (2008) Levels of truth: macro-truth and the TRC, in Chapman, A., and van der Merwe, H. (eds), *Truth and Reconciliation in South Africa: Did the TRC Deliver?* Philadelphia: University of Pennsylvania Press.

Chappell, L. (2012) The role of the ICC in transitional gender justice: capacity and limitations, in Buckley-Zistel, S., and Stanley, R. (eds), *Gender in Transitional Justice*. Basingstoke: Palgrave Macmillan.

Charlesworth, H. (1994) What are 'women's international human rights'? in Cook, R. J (ed.), *Human Rights of Women: National and International Perspectives*. Philadelphia: University of Pennsylvania Press.

Charlesworth, H. (1999) Feminist methods in international law, *American Journal of International Law*, 93(2): 379–94.

Christian Aid (2015) *Stand Strong: Women and Politics, Kailahun, Sierra Leone*, www.christianaid.org.uk/sites/default/files/2016-12/stand-strong-women-politics-report-assessment-kailahun-sierra-leone-nov-2015.pdf.

Clark, P. (2008) Law, politics and pragmatism: the ICC and case selection in Uganda and the Democratic Republic of Congo, in Waddell, N., and Clark, P. (eds), *Courting Conflict? Justice, Peace and the ICC in Africa*. London: Royal African Society.

Clark, P. (2010) *The Gacaca Courts, Post-Genocide Justice and Reconciliation in Rwanda*. Cambridge: Cambridge University Press.

Cole, C. M. (2014) At the convergence of transitional justice and art, *International Journal of Transitional Justice*, 8(2): 314–22.

Cole, E. A. (2017) *No Legacy for Transitional Justice Efforts without Education: Education as an Outreach Partner for Transitional Justice*. New York: International Center for Transitional Justice, www.ictj.org/sites/default/files/Transitional_Justice_Legacy_Education.pdf.

Conley-Zilkic, B., Brechenmacher, S., and Sarkar, A. (2016) *Assessing the Anti-Atrocity Toolbox*, World Peace Foundation Occasional Paper, http://fletcher.tufts.edu/~/media/Fletcher/Microsites/World%20Peace%20Foundation/Publications/Atrocity%20Toolbox_February%202016.pdf.

Cooper-Knock, S. J. (2016) Gender, politics and parliament in Rwanda, *Open Democracy*, 26 February, www.opendemocracy.net/westminster/sarah-jane-cooper-knock/gender-politics-and-parliament-in-rwanda.

Correa, C. (2013) *Reparations in Peru: From Recommendations to Implementation*. New York: International Center for Transitional Justice, www.ictj.org/sites/default/files/ICTJ_Report_Peru_Reparations_2013.pdf.

Cronin-Furman, K. (2013) Managing expectations: international criminal trials and the prospects for deterrence of mass atrocity, *International Journal of Transitional Justice*, 7(3): 434–54.

Dancy, G. (2010) Impact assessment, not evaluation: defining a limited role for positivism in the study of transitional justice, *International Journal of Transitional Justice*, 4(3): 355–76.

Dancy, G., and Wiebelhaus-Brahm, E. (2015) Bridge to human development or vehicle of inequality? Transitional justice and economic structures, *International Journal of Transitional Justice*, 9(1): 51–69.

Darcy, S. (2018) The principle of legality at the crossroads of human rights and international criminal law, in deGuzman, M. M., and Amann, D. M. (eds), *Arcs of Global Justice: Essays in Honour of William A. Schabas*. Oxford: Oxford University Press.

David, R. (2011) *Lustration and Transitional Justice: Personnel Systems in the Czech Republic, Hungary, and Poland*. Philadelphia: University of Pennsylvania Press.

de Greiff, P. (2008) Justice and reparations, in de Greiff, P. (ed.), *The Handbook of Reparations*. Oxford: Oxford University Press.

de Greiff, P. (2012) Theorizing transitional justice, *Nomos*, 51: 31–77.

de Greiff, P. (2014) On making the invisible visible: the role of cultural interventions in transitional justice processes, in Ramírez-Barat, C. (ed.), *Transitional Justice, Culture, and Society: Beyond Outreach*. New York: Social Science Research Council, Columbia University Press.

de Langis, T., and Studzinsky, S. (2012) *Briefing Paper on the ECCC, the Cambodian Women's Hearing, and Steps for Addressing Sexual Violence under the Khmer Rouge Regime*, http://gbvkr.org/wp-content/uploads/2013/02/Briefing-Paper-on-VAWECCC-Theresa-de-Langis-Final-ENG.pdf.

Democratic Progress Institute (2015) *Addressing Gender in Transitional Justice Mechanisms*, www.democraticprogress.org/wp-content/uploads/2016/01/Gender-in-Transitional-Justice-Mechanisms.pdf.

Doucet, A., and Mauthner, N. S. (2007) Feminist methodologies and epistemology, in Bryant, C. D., and Peck, D. L. (eds), *21st Century Sociology: A Reference Handbook*. Thousand Oaks, CA: Sage.

Drakulić, S. (2017) Playing to the audience: the televised suicide of Slobodan Praljak, *Eurozine*, 12 December, www.eurozine.com/playing-to-the-audience-the-televised-suicide-of-slobodan-praljak/.

Drexler, E. (2009) Addressing the legacies of mass violence and genocide in Indonesia and East Timor, in Hinton, A. L., and O'Neill, K. L. (eds), *Genocide: Truth, Memory, and Representation*. Durham, NC: Duke University Press.

Duggan, C. (2010a) 'Show me your impact': evaluating transitional justice in contested spaces, *Evaluation and Program Planning*, 35(1): 199–205.

Duggan, C. (2010b) Editorial note, *International Journal of Transitional Justice*, 4(3): 315–28.

Dumas, H., and Korman, R. (2011) Espaces de la mémoire du génocide des Tutsis au Rwanda: mémoriaux et lieux de mémoire, *Afrique Contemporaine*, 238(2): 11–27.

Elster, J. (2004) *Closing the Books: Transitional Justice in Historical Perspective*. Cambridge: Cambridge University Press.

Encarnación, O. G. (2015) *Democracy without Justice in Spain: The Politics of Forgetting*. Philadelphia: University of Pennsylvania Press.

Engstrom, P. (2013) Transitional justice and ongoing conflict, in Sriram, C. L., García-Godos, J., Herman, J., and Martin-Ortega, O. (eds), *Transitional Justice and Peacebuilding on the Ground: Victims and Ex-Combatants*. Abingdon: Routledge.

Engstrom, P. (2016) The inter-American human rights system and US–Latin American relations, in Scarfi, J. P., and Tillman, A. R.

(eds), *Cooperation and Hegemony in US–Latin American Relations*. Basingstoke: Palgrave Macmillan.

Engstrom, P. (forthcoming) Transitional justice and the inter-American human rights system in Latin America, *International Journal of Human Rights*.

Farasat, W., and Hayner, P. (2009) *Negotiating Peace in Nepal: Implications for Justice*. New York: International Center for Transitional Justice, https://ictj.org/sites/default/files/ICTJ-IFP-Nepal-Negotiating-Peace-2009-English.pdf.

Ford, S. (2013) Fairness and politics at the ICTY: evidence from the indictments, *North Carolina Journal of International Law and Commercial Regulation*, 39(1): 45–113.

Freedman, J. (2017) *A Conviction in Question: The First Trial at the International Criminal Court*. Toronto: University of Toronto Press.

Friedman, R. (2017) *Competing Memories: Truth and Reconciliation in Sierra Leone and Peru*. Cambridge: Cambridge University Press.

Fulu, E., Warner, X., Miedema, S., Jewkes, R., Roselli, T., and Lang, J. (2013) *Why Do Some Men Use Violence against Women and How Can We Prevent It? Quantitative Findings from the United Nations Multi-Country Study on Men and Violence in Asia and the Pacific*, www.partners4prevention.org/sites/default/files/resources/p4p-report.pdf.

Galtung, J. (1969) Violence, peace and peace research, *Journal of Peace Research*, 6(3): 167–91.

Galtung, J. (1990) Cultural violence, *Journal of Peace Research*, 27(3): 291–305.

García-Godos, J. (2012) Colombia: accountability and DDR in the pursuit of peace? in Sriram, C. L., García-Godos, J., Herman, J., and Martin-Ortega, O. (eds), *Transitional Justice and Peacebuilding on the Ground: Victims and Ex-Combatants*. Abingdon: Routledge.

García-Godos, J. (2016) Victims in focus, *International Journal of Transitional Justice*, 10(2): 350–8.

Gibson, J. L. (2004) Does truth lead to reconciliation? Testing the causal assumptions of the South African truth and reconciliation process, *American Journal of Political Science*, 48(2): 201–17.

Glasius, M. (2009) What is global justice and who decides? Civil society and victim responses to the International Criminal

Court's first investigations, *Human Rights Quarterly*, 31(2): 496–520.

Grace, K., and Eng, S. (2015) There is no place for 'chbab srey' in Cambodian schools, *Cambodia Daily*, 9 June, www. cambodiadaily.com/news/%C2%ADthere-is-no-place-for-chbab-srey-in-cambodian-schools-85230/.

Grandin, G. (2005) The instruction of great catastrophe: truth commissions, national history, and state formation in Argentina, Chile, and Guatemala, *American Historical Review*, 110(1): 46–67.

Grandin, G., and Klubock, T. M. (eds) (2007) *Truth Commissions: State Terror, History and Memory*, *Radical History*, 97 [special issue].

Gray, D. C. (2010) Extraordinary justice, *Alabama Law Review*, 62(1): 55–109.

Gready, P., and Robins, S. (2014) From transitional to transformative justice: a new agenda for practice, *International Journal of Transitional Justice*, 8(3): 339–61.

Gready, P., and Robins, S. (2017) Rethinking civil society and transitional justice: lessons from social movements and 'new' civil society, *International Journal of Human Rights*, 21(7): 956–75.

Grene, H., and Cammaer, R. (2017) *Out of the Frying Pan, into the Fire, Part One: Understanding the Links between Climate Change and Violent Conflict*, www.christianaid.org. uk/sites/default/files/2017-11/Out_of_the_frying_pan_part_1_ oct_2017.pdf.

Guereña, A. (2017) *A Snapshot of Inequality: What the Latest Agricultural Census Reveals about Land Distribution in Colombia*. Oxfam, www.oxfam.org/en/research/ snapshot-inequality.

Hansen, T. O., and Sriram, C. L. (2015) Fighting for justice (and survival): Kenyan civil society accountability strategies and their enemies, *International Journal of Transitional Justice*, 9(3): 407–27.

Hayner, P. (2010) *Unspeakable Truths: Transitional Justice and the Challenge of Truth Commissions*. 2nd edn, Abingdon: Routledge.

Hazan, P. (2006) Measuring the impact of punishment and forgiveness: a framework for evaluating transitional justice, *International Review of the Red Cross*, 88(861): 19–47.

Hobbs, H. (2016) Locating the logic of transitional justice in liberal democracies: native title in Australia, *University of New South Wales Law Journal*, 39(2): 512–52.

Hobbs, H. (2018) International criminal justice redux: a new wave of hybrid courts, *Justice in Conflict*, 13 March, https://justiceinconflict.org/2018/03/13/international-criminal-justice-redux-a-new-wave-of-hybrid-courts/.

Horne, C. M. (2014) Lustration, transitional justice, and social trust in post-communist countries: repairing or wresting the ties that bind? Europe-Asia Studies, 66(2): 225–54.

Horne, C. M. (2017) Transitional justice: vetting and lustration, in Lawther, C., Moffet, L., and Jacobs, D. (eds), Research Handbook on Transitional Justice. Cheltenham: Edward Elgar.

Human Rights Watch (2011) *Justice Compromised: The Legacy of Rwanda's Community-Based Gacaca Courts*, www.hrw.org/report/2011/05/31/justice-compromised/legacy-rwandas-community-based-gacaca-courts.

Huyse, L. (1995) Justice after transition: on the choices successor elites make in dealing with the past, *Law & Social Inquiry*, 20(1): 51–78.

Huyse, L. (2013) *Transitional Justice after War and Dictatorship: Learning from European Experiences (1945–2010): Final Report*. Brussels: CEGES-SOMA, www.cegesoma.be/docs/media/Recherche/TransJustFinalReport.pdf.

Hyvarinen, J. (2015) Respect and protect human rights: lessons from transitional justice, *Mary Robinson Foundation – Climate Justice*, www.mrfcj.org/wp-content/uploads/2015/09/JoyHyvarinen_Respectandprotecthumanrights_lessonsfromtransitionaljustice.pdf.

ICTJ (International Center for Transitional Justice) (2017) What is transitional justice? www.ictj.org/about/transitional-justice.

Igreja, V. (2015) Amnesty law, political struggles for legitimacy and violence in Mozambique, *International Journal of Transitional Justice*, 9(2): 239–58.

Impunity Watch (2013) Policy brief: guiding principles of memorialisation, www.impunitywatch.org/docs/Policy_Brief_Guiding_Principles_of_Memorialisation-2.pdf.

Ingelaere, B. (2008) The Gacaca courts in Rwanda, in Huyse, L., and Salter, M. (eds), *Traditional Justice and Reconciliation after Violent Conflict: Learning from African Experiences*. Stockholm: International IDEA.

Institute for Economics and Peace (2018) *Global Peace Index 2018: Measuring Peace in A Complex World*, http://visionofhumanity. org/app/uploads/2018/06/Global-Peace-Index-2018-2.pdf.

International Commission of Jurists (2017) Nepal: extending transitional justice commissions without granting real powers betrays trust of victims, 10 February, www.icj.org/ nepal-extending-transitional-justice-commissions-without-granting-real-powers-will-once-again-betray-trust-of-victims/.

Judt, T. (2005) *Postwar: A History of Europe since 1945*. London: Heinemann.

Kaufman, J. P. (2016) Women and children, war and peace: political agency in time of conflict, *International Affairs*, 92(6): 1499–504.

Kelly, L., Regan, L., and Burton, S. (1992) Defending the indefensible? Quantitative methods and feminist research, in Hinds, H., Phoenix, A., and Stacey, J. (eds), *Working Out: New Directions for Women's Studies*. London: Falmer Press.

Kemp, S. (2014) Guatemala prosecutes former President Ríos Montt: new perspectives on genocide and domestic criminal justice, *Journal of International Criminal Justice*, 12(1): 133–56.

Kerr, R., and Mobekk, E. (2007) *Peace and Justice: Seeking Accountability after War*. Cambridge: Polity.

Kersten, M. (2016) *Justice in Conflict: The Effects of the International Criminal Court's Interventions on Ending Wars and Building Peace*. Oxford: Oxford University Press.

Kersten, M. (2017) How three words could change the ICC–Africa relationship, *Justice in Conflict*, 9 May, https://justiceinconflict. org/2017/05/09/how-three-words-could-change-the-icc-africa-relationship/.

Kersten, M. (2018) As the pendulum swings – the revival of the hybrid tribunal, in Christensen, M. J., and Levi, R. (eds), *International Practices of Criminal Justice: Social and Legal Perspectives*. Abingdon: Routledge.

Kingdom of Cambodia, Ministry of Women's Affairs (2005) *Cambodia Report* for the Ten-year Review and Appraisal of the Implementation of the Beijing Declaration and Platform for Action (1995) and the outcomes of the Twenty-third Special Session of the General Assembly (2000), www.unescapsdd.org/ files/images/Beijing20_national_review_Cambodia.pdf.

Kovras, I. (2017) *Grassroots Activism and the Evolution of*

Transitional Justice: The Families of the Disappeared. Cambridge: Cambridge University Press.

Lambourne, W. (2009) Transitional justice and peacebuilding after mass violence, *International Journal of Transitional Justice*, 3(1): 28–48.

Lanegran, K. (2015) The Kenyan Truth, Justice and Reconciliation Commission: the importance of commissioners and their appointment process, *Transitional Justice Review*, 1(3): 41–71.

Lanni, A. (2014) Transitional justice in ancient Athens: a case study, *University of Pennsylvania Journal of International Law*, 32(2): 551–94.

Laplante, L. J. (2008) Transitional justice and peace building: diagnosing and addressing the socioeconomic roots of violence through a human rights framework, *International Journal of Transitional Justice*, 2(3): 331–55.

Laplante, L. J. (2009a) Outlawing amnesty: the return of criminal justice in transitional justice schemes, *Virginia Journal of International Law*, 49(4): 915–84.

Laplante, L. J. (2009b) From theory to practice: implementing reparations in post-truth commission Peru, in Johnston, B. R., and Slyomovics, S. (eds), *Waging War, Making Peace: Reparations and Human Rights*. Walnut Creek, CA: Left Coast Press.

Leebaw, B. A. (2008) The irreconcilable goals of transitional justice, *Human Rights Quarterly*, 30(1)L 35–118.

Leebaw, B. A. (2012) Review of Kathryn Sikkink's *The Justice Cascade: How Human Rights Prosecutions are Changing World Politics*, *Journal of Human Rights*, 11(2): 301–7.

Leroy, M. (2009) *Environment, Climate Change and Conflict in Africa: Reflections on Darfur*. Costa Rica: University for Peace.

Levi, P. (1989) *The Drowned and the Saved*. New York: Vintage Books.

Lie, T. G., Binningsbø, H. M., and Gates, S. (2007) *Post-Conflict Justice and Sustainable Peace*, World Bank Policy Research Working Paper 4191, http://siteresources.worldbank.org/INTLAWJUSTINST/Resources/PostConflict.pdf.

Longman, T. (2017) *Memory and Justice in Post-Genocide Rwanda*. Cambridge: Cambridge University Press.

Lundy, P., and McGovern, M. (2008) Whose justice? Rethinking transitional justice from the bottom up, *Journal of Law and Society*, 35(2): 265–92.

McAuliffe, P. (2013a) Romanticization versus integration? Indigenous justice in rule of law reconstruction and transitional justice discourse, *Goettingen Journal of International Law*, 5(1): 41–86.

McAuliffe, P. (2013b) The roots of transitional accountability: interrogating the 'justice cascade', *International Journal of Law in Context*, 9(1): 106–23.

McAuliffe, P. (2014) Ariel Dorfman's *Death and the Maiden* as a mirror reflecting the dilemmas of transitional justice policy, in Rush, P. D., and Simić, O. (eds), *The Arts of Transitional Justice: Culture, Activism, and Memory after Atrocity*. New York: Springer.

McAuliffe, P. (2017) *Transformative Transitional Justice and the Malleability of Post-Conflict States*. Cheltenham: Edward Elgar.

McCargo, D. (2011) Politics by other means? The virtual trials of the Khmer Rouge tribunal, *International Affairs*, 87(3): 613–27.

Macdonald, A. (2015) From the ground up: what does the evidence tell us about local experiences of transitional justice? *Transitional Justice Review*, 1(3): 72–121.

McEvoy, K., and McConnachie, K. (2013) Victims and transitional justice: voice, agency and blame, *Social and Legal Studies*, 22(4): 489–513.

McGregor, R. (2017) *Asia's Reckoning: China, Japan, the US and the Struggle for Global Power*. London: Allen Lane.

Madlingozi, T. (2010) On transitional justice entrepreneurs and the production of victims, *Journal of Human Rights Practice*, 13(2): 208–28.

Magarrell, L. (2003) Reparations for massive or widespread human rights violations: sorting out claims for reparations and social justice, *Windsor Yearbook of Access to Justice*, 22: 85.

Mageza-Barthel, R. (2012) Asserting their presence! Women's quest for transitional justice in post-genocide Rwanda, in Buckley-Zistel, S., and Stanley, R. (eds), *Gender in Transitional Justice*. Basingstoke: Palgrave Macmillan.

Mageza-Barthel, R. (2015) *Mobilizing Transnational Gender Politics in Post-Genocide Rwanda*. Abingdon: Routledge.

Mahony, C. (2015) A political tool? The politics of case selection at the special court for Sierra Leone, in Ainley, K., Friedman, R., and Mahony, C. (eds), *Evaluating Transitional Justice: Accountability and Peacebuilding in Post-Conflict Sierra Leone*. Basingstoke: Palgrave Macmillan.

Malca, C. G. (2015) Peru: changing contexts for transitional justice, in Skaar, E., Malca, C. G., and Eide, T., *After Violence: Transitional Justice, Peace and Democracy*. Abingdon: Routledge.

Mallinder, L. (2007) Can amnesties and international justice be reconciled? *International Journal of Transitional Justice*, 1(2): 208–30.

Mallinder, L. (2008) *Amnesty, Human Rights and Political Transitions: Bridging the Peace and Justice Divide*. Oxford: Hart.

Mam, K. (2004) The endurance of the Cambodian family under the Khmer Rouge regime: an oral history, in Cook, S. (ed.) *Genocide in Cambodia and Rwanda: New Perspectives*. New Brunswick, NJ: Transaction.

Mamdani, M. (1996) Reconciliation without justice, *South African Review of Books*, 46.

Mamdani, M. (2009) *Saviors and Survivors: Darfur, Politics, and the War on Terror*. New York: Verso.

Mani, R. (2002) *Beyond Retribution: Justice in the Shadow of War*. Cambridge: Polity.

Mani, R. (2005) Rebuilding an inclusive political community after war, *Security Dialogue*, 36(4): 511–26.

Mani, R., and Kelly, W. (2017) *The Gift of Peace*, Theatre of Transformation Academy, http://theatreoftransformation.org/the-gift-of-peace-2/.

Marks, S. P., and Naraharisetti, R. (2013) Cambodia: civil society, power and stalled democracy, in Andreassen, B. A., and Crawford, G. (eds), *Human Rights, Power and Civic Action: Comparative Analyses of Struggles for Rights in Developing Societies*. Abingdon: Routledge.

Marrus, M. R. (2007) Official apologies and the quest for historical justice, *Journal of Human Rights*, 6(1): 75–105.

Mayer-Rieckh, A., and de Greiff, P. (eds) (2007) *Justice as Prevention: Vetting Public Employees in Transitional Societies*. New York: Social Science Research Council.

Mendeloff, D. (2004) Truth-seeking, truth-telling, and postconflict peacebuilding: curb the enthusiasm? *International Studies Review*, 6(3): 355–80.

Mendes, E. (2010) *Peace and Justice at the International Criminal Court: A Court of Last Resort*. Cheltenham: Edward Elgar.

Mertus, J. (2004) Shouting from the bottom of the well: the impact of international trials for wartime rape on women's agency, *International Feminist Journal of Politics*, 6(1): 110–28.

Miller, Z. (2008) Effects of invisibility: in search of the 'economic' in transitional justice, *International Journal of Transitional Justice*, 2(3): 266–91.

Minow, M (1998) *Between Vengeance and Forgiveness*. Boston: Beacon Press.

Mohan, M. (2009) The paradox of victim-centrism: victim participation at the Khmer Rouge tribunal, *International Criminal Law Review*, 9(5): 1–43.

Moore, L. M. (2009) (Re)covering the past, remembering the trauma: the politics of commemoration at sites of atrocity, *Journal of Public and International Affairs*, 20(spring): 47–64.

Moreno-Ocampo, L. M. (2008) Building a future on peace and justice: the International Criminal Court, in Ambos, K., Large, J. and Wierda, M. (eds), *Building a Future on Peace and Justice: Studies on Transitional Justice, Peace and Development*. New York: Springer.

Murphy, C. (2016) Transitional justice, in Watene, K., and Drydyk, J. (eds), *Theorizing Justice: Critical Insights and Future Directions*. New York: Rowman & Littlefield International.

Murphy, C. (2017) *The Conceptual Foundations of Transitional Justice*. Cambridge: Cambridge University Press.

Nagy, R. (2008) Transitional justice as global project: critical reflections, *Third World Quarterly*, 29(2): 275–89.

Naughton, E. (2016a) Kenya: case study, pp. 57–71 in *Challenging the Conventional: Can Truth Commissions Strengthen Peace Processes?* ICTJ/Kofi Annan Foundation, www.ictj.org/publication/challenging-conventional-can-truth-commissions-strengthen-peace-processes.

Naughton, E. (2016b) Nepal: case study, pp. 72–81 in *Challenging the Conventional: Can Truth Commissions Strengthen Peace Processes?* ICTJ/Kofi Annan Foundation, www.ictj.org/publication/challenging-conventional-can-truth-commissions-strengthen-peace-processes.

Nesiah, V. (2016) *Transitional Justice Practice: Looking Back, Moving Forward*. Utrecht: Impunity Watch, www.impunitywatch.org/docs/scoping_study_FINAL1.pdf.

Neufeldt, R. C. (2007)*'Frameworkers' and 'Circlers' – Exploring Assumptions in Peace and Conflict Impact Assessment*. Berlin: Berghof Research Center for Constructive Conflict Management,

www.berghof-foundation.org/fileadmin/redaktion/Publications/
Handbook/Articles/neufeldt_handbook.pdf.

Newman, M. (2016) *Six Authors in Search of Justice: Engaging with Political Transitions*. London: Hurst.

Ní Aoláin, F. (2000) Sex-based violence and the Holocaust: a reevaluation of harms and rights in international law, *Yale Journal of Law and Feminism*, 12: 43–84.

Ní Aoláin, F. (2012a) Gendered under-enforcement in the transitional justice context, in Buckley-Zistel, S., and Stanley, R. (eds), *Gender in Transitional Justice*. Basingstoke: Palgrave Macmillan.

Ní Aoláin, F. (2012b) Advancing feminist positioning in the field of transitional justice, *International Journal of Transitional Justice*, 6(2): 205–28.

Niner, S. (2017) *Iha lalehan nia klaran no rai* – living between heaven and earth: understanding *jender* in Timor-Leste, in Niner, S. (ed.), *Women and the Politics of Gender in Post-Conflict Timor-Leste*. Abingdon: Routledge.

Novick, P. (1968) *The Resistance versus Vichy: The Purge of Collaborators in Liberated France*. London: Chatto & Windus.

Nussbaum, M. (2016) *Anger and Forgiveness: Resentment, Generosity, and Justice*. Oxford: Oxford University Press.

OECD (Organisation for Economic Co-operation and Development) (2007) *Enhancing the Delivery of Justice and Security: Governance, Peace and Security*, www.oecd.org/dac/conflict-fragility-resilience/docs/38434642.pdf.

Olsen, T. D., Payne, L. A., and Reiter, A. G. (2010a) *Transitional Justice in Balance: Comparing Processes, Weighing Efficacy*. Washington, DC: United States Institute of Peace Press.

Olsen, T. D., Payne, L. A., and Reiter, A. G. (2010b) The justice balance: when transitional justice improves human rights and democracy, *Human Rights Quarterly*, 32(4): 980–1007.

Oosterveld, V. (2015) Sexual and gender-based violence in post-conflict Sierra Leone: the contribution of transitional justice mechanisms to domestic law reform, in Ainley, K., Friedman, R., and Mahony, C. (eds), *Evaluating Transitional Justice: Accountability and Peacebuilding in Post-Conflict Sierra Leone*. Basingstoke: Palgrave Macmillan.

Oosterveld, V., and Sellers, P. (2016) Issues of sexual and gender-based violence at the ECCC, in Meisenberg S. M., and

Stegmiller, I. (eds), *The Extraordinary Chambers in the Courts of Cambodia*. The Hague: T.M.C. Asser Press.

Ormhaug, C. M., Meier, P., and Hernes, H. (2009) *Armed Conflict Deaths Disaggregated by Gender*. Oslo: International Peace Research Institute.

O'Rourke, C. (2012) Transitioning to what? Transitional justice and gendered citizenship in Chile and Colombia, in Buckley-Zistel, S., and Stanley, R. (eds), *Gender in Transitional Justice*. Basingstoke: Palgrave Macmillan.

O'Rourke, C. (2013) *Gender Politics in Transitional Justice*. Abingdon: Routledge.

Osiel, M. (2000) Why prosecute? Critics of punishment for mass atrocity, *Human Rights Quarterly*, 22(1): 118–47.

Ottendoerfer, E. (2018) Outreach, in-reach or beyond reach? Lessons learned from hybrid courts, *Justice in Conflict*, 15 March, https://justiceinconflict.org/2018/03/15/outreach-in-reach-or-beyond-reach-lessons-learned-from-hybrid-courts/.

Pelizzon, A. (2015) Transitional justice and ecological jurisprudence in the midst of an ever-changing climate, in Szablewska, N., and Bachmann, S.-D. (eds), *Current Issues in Transitional Justice: Towards a More Holistic Approach*. New York: Springer.

Peters, F. (2016) Remaking Polish national history: reenactment over reflection, *Cultures of History Forum*, 3 October, www.cultures-of-history.uni-jena.de/politics/poland/remaking-polish-national-history-reenactment-over-reflection/.

Pham, P., and Vinck, P. (2010) *Transitioning to Peace: A Population-Based Survey on Attitudes about Social Reconstruction and Justice in Northern Uganda*. Berkeley: Human Rights Center, University of California, www.law.berkeley.edu/files/HRC/Publications_Transitioning-to-Peace_12-2010.pdf.

Pham, P., Vinck, P., Balthazard, M., Hean, S., and Stover, E. (2009) *So We Will Never Forget: A Population-Based Survey on Attitudes about Social Reconstruction and the Extraordinary Chambers in the Courts of Cambodia*. Berkeley: Human Rights Center, University of California, http://hhi.harvard.edu/sites/default/files/publications/so-we-will-never-forget.pdf.

Philpott, D. (2012) *Just and Unjust Peace: An Ethic of Political Reconciliation*. Oxford: Oxford University Press.

Picker, R. (2005) *Victims' Perspectives about the Human Rights Violations Hearings*, Centre for the Study of Violence and Reconciliation, https://csvr.org.za/docs/humanrights/ victimsperspectivshearings.pdf.

Pigou, P. (2004) *The Community Reconciliation Process of the Commission for Reception, Truth and Reconciliation*, United Nations Development Programme, http://citeseerx.ist.psu.edu/ viewdoc/download?doi=10.1.1.737.3841&rep=rep1&type=pdf.

Porter, E. (2012) Gender-inclusivity in transitional justice strategies: women in Timor-Leste, in Buckley-Zistel, S, and Stanley, R. (eds), *Gender in Transitional Justice*. Basingstoke: Palgrave Macmillan.

Posner, E. A., and Vermeule, A. (2003) Transitional justice as ordinary justice, *Harvard Law Review*, 117: 762–825.

Ramírez-Barat, C. (ed.) (2014) *Transitional Justice, Culture, and Society: Beyond Outreach*. New York: Social Science Research Council.

Razack, S. H. (2007) Stealing the pain of others: reflections on Canadian humanitarian responses, *Review of Education, Pedagogy, and Cultural Studies*, 29(4): 375–94.

Reátegui, F. (2016) Guatemala: case study, pp. 24–31 in *Challenging the Conventional: Can Truth Commissions Strengthen Peace Processes?* ICTJ/Kofi Annan Foundation www.ictj.org/ publication/challenging-conventional-can-truth-commissions-strengthen-peace-processes.

Reiter, A. G., and Surian, K. Z. (2015) Research note – transitional justice in higher education: assessing the state of the field, *Transitional Justice Review*, 1(3): 122–31.

Rieff, D. (2016) *In Praise of Forgetting*. New Haven, CT: Yale University Press.

Roach, S. C. (2016) South Sudan: a volatile dynamic of accountability and peace, *International Affairs*, 92(6): 1343–59.

Robins, S. (2011) Towards victim-centred transitional justice: understanding the needs of families of the disappeared in postconflict Nepal, *International Journal of Transitional Justice*, 5(1): 75–98.

Robins, S. (2012) Challenging the therapeutic ethic: a victim-centred evaluation of transitional justice process in Timor-Leste, *International Journal of Transitional Justice*, 6(1): 83–105.

Robins, S. (2013) Toward victim-centered transitional justice: Nepal and Timor-Leste, *Middle East Institute*, www.mei.edu/ content/toward-victim-centered-transitional-justice-nepal-and-timor-leste.

Ross, F. C. (2010) An acknowledged failure: women, voice, violence, and the South African Truth and Reconciliation Commission, in Shaw, R., and Waldorf, L., with Hazan, P. (eds), *Localizing Transitional Justice: Interventions and Priorities after Mass Violence*. Stanford, CA: Stanford University Press.

Rothenberg, D. (2016) *Memory of Silence: The Guatemalan Truth Commission Report*. Basingstoke: Palgrave Macmillan.

Rowbotham, S. (1973) *Hidden from History: 300 Years of Women's Oppression and the Fight against it*. London: Pluto Press.

Rowen, J. (2017) *Searching for Truth in the Transitional Justice Movement*. Cambridge: Cambridge University Press.

Rubio-Marín, R. (2006) The gender of reparations: setting the agenda, in Rubio-Marín, R. (ed.), *What Happened to the Women? Gender and Reparations for Human Rights Violations*. New York: Social Science Research Council.

Rush, P., and Simić, O. (eds) (2014) *The Arts of Transitional Justice: Culture, Activism, and Memory after Atrocity*. New York: Springer.

Salvá, A. (2016) Domestic violence in Cambodia, *The Diplomat*, 15 April, https://thediplomat.com/2016/04/domestic-violence-in-cambodia/.

Sankey, D. (2016) Recognition of gendered experiences of harm at the extraordinary chambers in the courts of Cambodia: the promise and the pitfalls, *Feminist Legal Studies*, 24(1): 7–27.

Schabas, W. (2012) *Unimaginable Atrocities: Justice, Politics, and Rights at the War Crimes Tribunals*. Oxford: Oxford University Press.

Scharf, M. (2004) Perspectives on the future: the amnesty exception to the jurisdiction of the International Criminal Court, in Bekou, O., and Cryer, R. (eds), *The International Criminal Court*. Aldershot: Ashgate.

Sen, A. (2009) *The Idea of Justice*. London: Allen Lane.

Sharp, D. N. (2015) Emancipating transitional justice from the bonds of the paradigmatic transition, *International Journal of Transitional Justice*, 9(1): 150–69.

Shaw, R., and Waldorf, L. (2010) Introduction: localizing transitional justice, in Shaw, R., and Waldorf, L., with Hazan, P. (eds), *Localizing Transitional Justice: Interventions and Priorities after Mass Violence*. Stanford, CA: Stanford University Press.

Sigsworth, R., and Valji, N. (2012) Continuities of violence against women in South Africa, in Buckley-Zistel, S., and Stanley, R. (eds), *Gender in Transitional Justice*. Basingstoke: Palgrave Macmillan.

Sikkink, K. (2011) *The Justice Cascade: How Human Rights Prosecutions are Changing World Politics*. New York: W. W. Norton.

Simpson, G. (2007) *Law, War and Crime*. Cambridge: Polity.

Sissons, M., and Al-Saiedi, A. (2013) *A Bitter Legacy: Lessons of De-Baathification in Iraq*. New York: International Center for Transitional Justice.

Sivac-Bryant, S. (2015) The Omarska memorial project as an example of how transitional justice interventions can produce hidden harms, *International Journal of Transitional Justice*, 9(1): 170–80.

Skaar, E. (2015) Uruguay: reconstructing peace and democracy through transitional justice, in Skaar, E., Malca, C. G., and Eide, T., *After Violence: Transitional Justice, Peace, and Democracy*. Abingdon: Routledge.

Skaar, E., Malca, C. G., and Eide, T. (2015) *After Violence: Transitional Justice, Peace, and Democracy*. Abingdon: Routledge.

Snyder, J., and Vinjamuri, L. (2003–4) Trials and errors: principle and pragmatism in strategies of international justice, *International Security*, 28(3): 5–44.

Sriram, C. L. (2007) Justice as peace? Liberal peacebuilding and strategies of transitional justice, *Global Society*, 21(4): 579–91.

Studzinsky, S. (2012) Neglected crimes: the challenge of raising sexual and gender-based crimes before the extraordinary chambers in the courts of Cambodia, in Buckley-Zistel, S., and Stanley, R. (eds), *Gender in Transitional Justice*. Basingstoke: Palgrave Macmillan.

Subotić, J. (2009) *Hijacked Justice: Dealing with the Past in the Balkans*. Ithaca, NY: Cornell University Press.

Subotić, J. (2011) Expanding the scope of post-conflict justice: individual, state and societal responsibility for mass atrocity, *Journal of Peace Research*, 48(2): 157–69.

Subotić, J. (2012) The transformation of international transitional justice advocacy, *International Journal of Transitional Justice*, 6(1): 106–25.

Swaine, A. (2018) *Conflict-Related Violence against Women:*

Transforming Transition. Cambridge: Cambridge University Press.

Szablewska, N., and Bachmann, S.-D. (2015) Current issues and future challenges in transitional justice, in Szablewska, N., and Bachmann, S.-D. (eds), *Current Issues in Transitional Justice: Towards a More Holistic Approach*. New York: Springer.

Tabak, S. (2011) False dichotomies of transitional justice: gender, conflict and combatants in Colombia, *New York University Journal of International Law and Politics*, 44: 103–64.

Taylor, D. (2014) *Victim Participation in Transitional Justice Mechanisms: Real Power or Empty Ritual?* Utrecht, Impunity Watch, www.impunitywatch.org/docs/IW_Discussion_Paper_Victim_Participation1.pdf.

Teale, L. (2009) *Addressing Gender-Based Violence in the Sierra Leone Conflict: Notes from the Field*, African Centre for the Constructive Resolution of Disputes, www.accord.org.za/ajcr-issues/%EF%BF%BCaddressing-gender-based-violence-in-the-sierra-leone-conflict/.

Teitel, R. (2000) *Transitional Justice*. Oxford: Oxford University Press.

Teitel, R. (2003) Transitional justice genealogy, *Harvard Human Rights Journal*, 16: 69–94.

Teitel, R. (2005) The law and politics of contemporary transitional justice, *Cornell International Law Journal*, 38(3): 837–62.

Teitel, R. (2010) *Global Transitional Justice*, Project on Human Rights, Global Justice and Democracy, Working Paper no. 8, George Mason University, www.gmu.edu/centers/globalstudies/publications/hjd/hjd_wp_8.pdf.

Theidon, K. (2009) Editorial note, *International Journal of Transitional Justice*, 3(3): 295–300.

Theidon, K. (2010) Histories of innocence: post-war stories in Peru, in Shaw, R., and Waldorf, L., with Hazan, P. (eds), *Localizing Transitional Justice: Interventions and Priorities after Mass Violence*. Stanford, CA: Stanford University Press.

Thoms, O. N. T., Ron, J., and Paris, R. (2008) *The Effects of Transitional Justice Mechanisms: A Summary of Empirical Research Findings and Implications for Analysts and Practitioners*, Centre for International Policy Studies, University of Ottawa, http://aix1.uottawa.ca/~rparis/CIPS_Transitional_Justice_April2008.pdf.

Tighe, C. (2016) Lustration – the Polish experience, *Journal of European Studies*, 46(3–4): 338–73.

Turner, C. (2016) *Violence, Law and the Impossibility of Transitional Justice*. Abingdon: Routledge.

UN (2004) *The Rule of Law and Transitional Justice in Conflict and Post-Conflict Societies*, Report of the Secretary-General, https://reliefweb.int/report/world/rule-law-and-transitional-justice-conflict-and-post-conflict-societies-report-secretary.

UN (2005) *Basic Principles and Guidelines on the Right to a Remedy and Reparation for Victims of Gross Violations of International Human Rights Law and Serious Violations of International Humanitarian Law* (General Assembly Resolution 60/147), www.legal-tools.org/doc/bcf508/pdf/.

UN (2009) *Report of the Office of the United Nations High Commissioner for Human Rights on the Relationship between Climate Change and Human Rights*, A/HRC/10/61, www.ohchr.org/Documents/Press/AnalyticalStudy.pdf.

UN (2011) *The Rule of Law and Transitional Justice in Conflict and Post-Conflict Societies*, Report of the Secretary-General, https://reliefweb.int/report/world/rule-law-and-transitional-justice-conflict-and-post-conflict-societies-report-secreta-0.

UN (2012a) *Report of the Special Rapporteur on the Promotion of Truth, Justice, Reparation and Guarantees of Non-Recurrence*, A/HRC/21/46, www.ohchr.org/Documents/HRBodies/HRCouncil/RegularSession/Session21/A-HRC-21-46_en.pdf.

UN (2012b) *Women's Participation in Peace Negotiations: Connections between Presence and Influence*, https://reliefweb.int/sites/reliefweb.int/files/resources/03AWomenPeaceNeg.pdf.

UN (2013) *General Recommendation no. 30 on Women in Conflict Prevention, Conflict and Post-Conflict Situations*, CEDAW/C/GC/30, www.refworld.org/docid/5268d2064.html.

UN (2014a) *Promotion of Truth, Justice, Reparation and Guarantees of Non-Recurrence*, Report of the Special Rapporteur, A/69/518, http://undocs.org/A/69/518.

UN (2014b) *Report of the Special Rapporteur in the Field of Cultural Rights: Memorialization Processes*, A/HRC/25/49, www.concernedhistorians.org/content_files/file/TO/328.pdf.

UNDP (2014) *Leaders: Women in Public Decision-Making and Politics: Cambodia Gender Assessment*, Policy Brief 8, www.kh.undp.org/content/dam/cambodia/docs/DemoGov/NearyRattanak4/Neary%20Rattanak%204%20-%20

Women%20in%20Public%20Decision-Making%20and%20 Politics_Eng.pdf.

UNDP (2018) *Human Development Indices and Indicators: 2018 Statistical Update*, www.hdr.undp.org/sites/default/files/2018_ human_development_statistical_update.pdf.

UNHCR (2017) Forced displacement growing in Colombia despite peace agreement, 10 March, www.unhcr.org/uk/news/ briefing/2017/3/58c26e114/forced-displacement-growing-colombia-despite-peace-agreement.html.

UNICEF (2009) *'Traditional' Justice Systems in the Pacific, Indonesia and Timor-Leste*, www.unicef.org/tdad/index_56512. html.

Valji, N. (2012)*A Window of Opportunity: Making Transitional Justice Work for Women*, UN Entity for Gender Equality and the Empowerment of Women, www.unwomen. org/~/media/Headquarters/Attachments/Sections/Library/ Publications/2012/10/06B-Making-Transitional-Justice-Work-for-Women.pdf.

van der Merwe, H. (2008) What survivors say about justice: an analysis of the TRC victim hearings, in Chapman, A. R., and van der Merwe, H. (eds), *Truth and Reconciliation in South Africa: Did the TRC Deliver?* Philadelphia: University of Pennsylvania Press.

van Nievelt, M. A. (2016) Transitional justice in ongoing conflict: Colombia's integrative approach to peace and justice, *Cornell International Affairs Review*, 9(2).

Vinck, P., and Pham, P. (2008) Ownership and participation in transitional justice, *International Journal of Transitional Justice*, 2(3): 398–411.

Wade, C. J. (2016) *Captured Peace: Elites and Peacebuilding in El Salvador*. Athens: Ohio University Press.

Waldorf, L. (2006) Mass justice for mass atrocity: rethinking local justice as transitional justice, *Temple Law Review*, 79(1) 1–87.

Waldorf, L. (2012) Anticipating the past: transitional justice and socio-economic wrongs, *Social and Legal Studies*, 2(2): 171–86.

Walker, M. U. (2016) Transformative reparations? A critical look at a current trend in thinking about gender-just reparations, *International Journal of Transitional Justice*, 10(1): 108–25.

Watts, J., and Vidal, J. (2017) Environmental defenders being killed in record numbers globally, new research reveals, *The Guardian*, 13 July, www.theguardian.com/environment/2017/

jul/13/environmental-defenders-being-killed-in-record-numbers-globally-new-research-reveals.

Wegner, P. S. (2015) *The International Criminal Court in Ongoing Intrastate Conflicts: Navigating the Peace–Justice Divide.* Cambridge: Cambridge University Press.

Weinstein, H. M., Fletcher, L. E., Vinck, P., and Pham, P. N. (2010) Stay the hand of justice: whose priorities take priority? in Shaw, R., and Waldorf, L., with Hazan, P. (eds), *Localizing Transitional Justice: Interventions and Priorities after Mass Violence.* Stanford, CA: Stanford University Press.

Westmarland, N. (2001) The quantitative/qualitative debate and feminist research: a subjective view of objectivity, *Forum: Qualitative Social Research*, 2(1), www.qualitative-research.net/index.php/fqs/article/view/974/2124.

Wiebelhaus-Brahm, E. (2009) What is a truth commission and why does it matter? *Peace and Conflict Review*, 3(2): 1–14.

Wiebelhaus-Brahm, E. (2010) *Truth Commissions and Transitional Societies: The Impact on Human Rights and Democracy.* Abingdon: Routledge.

Williams, M., and Nagy, R. (2012) Introduction: transitional justice, *Nomos*, 51: 1–30.

Winter, S. (2014) *Transitional Justice in Established Democracies.* Basingstoke: Palgrave Macmillan.

World Bank (2018)The World Bank in Timor-Leste, www.worldbank.org/en/country/timor-leste/overview.

Index

Index